RISE OF THE SEER PROPHETS

RISE OF THE SEER PROPHETS

Intimate Mysteries for a New Generation of Prophets

KURSHIN JOSEPH

Kurshin Joseph

Rise of The Seer Prophets

Copyright © Kurshin Joseph

All Rights Reserved.

No part of this book may be reproduced without written permission from the publisher.

PUBLISHED BY KURSHIN JOSEPH

For all enquiries and additional resources please go to www.kurshin-joseph.com

Scripture taken from the New King James Version®. Copyright © 1982 by Thomas Nelson. Used by permission. All rights reserved.

Scripture quotations taken from The Holy Bible, New International Version® NIV® Copyright © 1973 1978 1984 2011 by Biblica, Inc. ™ Used by permission. All rights reserved worldwide.

Ebook ISBN 978-0-6488442-0-4

Paperback ISBN 978-0-6488442-1-1

Mp3 Audio File ISBN 978-0-6488442-2-8

For Worldwide Distribution, Printed In Multiple International Locations. Published in 2020.

Dedication

I DEDICATE THIS BOOK TO THE ONE THAT SPARED MY LIFE AND COUNTED IT NECESSARY FOR ME TO BE PLACED IN THIS EXACT MOMENT IN TIME, THE MOST INTIMATE MYSTERY OF ALL, JESUS CHRIST. You are the love of my life, the Eternal Life, Healer & Provider whom I surrender to. You are the Joy set before me and the reason I do everything that I do. I pray that You are glorified. Thank You my beautiful Saviour King and Lord Jesus Christ.

I am truly Yours, I Love You.

Contents

1	Introduction	1
2	Desiring More	7
3	Levels Of Intimacy And Relationship	17
4	A Prophet's Authority	31
5	The Power Of Words As Frequency	45
6	Interpreting The Prophetic	55
7	Strongholds and Hindrances	67
8	Keys To Growing Prophetic Insight	79
9	A Prophet's Toolbox	99
10	Engaging The Secret Place	115
11	Conclusion	129
12	Bonus Chapter: The Latter Rain Church	131

I

Introduction

We are no longer in the last days, but in fact the last hour. Time is almost up and the demand for a harvest is more needed than ever. We must live by the spirit and save as many as we can. God is pouring out His Spirit on all flesh (Joel 2:28, Acts 2:17) because we can't get the job done ourselves. We need the Lord to work in the hearts of men, young and old, to receive dreams and visions of Jesus so that when we speak, they already have a seed inside of them from God. If today's prophets don't turn up with the power of the Kingdom of God, they will seek it elsewhere. So more than ever, prophets get ready to behold the Lord in a way that you never thought possible!

For the Kingdom of God is not a matter of talk but of power (1 Corinthians 4:20 NIV).

The Lord began speaking to me about the necessity to see into Kingdom realms and operate from Heaven to Earth. It is no longer sufficient to have the gospel without true, authentic demonstrations and experiential knowledge of the word of God, especially for Prophets. The Lord will always confirm His Word with tangible signs and wonders coming out from the Kingdom dimensions. The occult world has been doing similar phenomena for a long time, but the church has failed to operate in greater dimensions. Yet Jesus gave us the authority of Heaven, not to the demons and false religious systems. We as spiritual beings on Earth are to bear witness to the will of God, bearing His image and are desperately needed to manifest as sons of God and take the positions of our rightful inheritance and that is to represent the government of Heaven. We need to learn to operate as spirits and no longer mere mortals tied to a physical body. The Earth was subjected to chaos due to the sin of man, but restoration is our duty as manifested sons of God. It is for restoration sake and for the sake of expansion of the Heavenly reality which our Creator originally intended. Consider, what is the point of only getting to Heaven one day and just trying not to sin in the meantime? You may as well accept the blood covenant of Jesus for the redemption of your sin and then roll over dead. But that is not the case, we were left on this earth to govern this world from a glorified state in Christ. Adam and Eve were to take care of the earth while operating out of Heaven. We got locked out of Heaven because God needed to contain sin within 'time'. The original purpose was to make earth look like what Heaven does, so that Heaven could expand its dominion into this domain. Adam originally functioned in Heaven and earth at the same time. This was proven by quantum physics explaining that we have different consciences in other dimensions or planes of frequencies. Being in two locations at once is called duality which is happening right now, but we are unable to perceive it due to the unrenewed mind. But the truth is we have been seated in Heavenly places with Christ, but we can't see it. This is why it is essential for Seer Prophets to begin to expound wisdom of what is seen in Kingdom Realms and to begin to teach others how to see and activate them. It is our original sight that I am speaking of. It is not something new, it is simply returning to what we had before the fall of man and coming to earth. Up until now we have been only hearing the voice of the Lord as an inner witness as a general rule of thumb for the church. However, if we do not begin to see what our Heavenly Father does and do as He did, we will never come to maturity as Jesus showed us by example.

This book may have several controversial topics, so whatever understanding you can get from it, please take it before God because everyone's journey may be at different stages. I have so much more to learn about the Kingdom of God, but the Lord has pressed me to write with the expectation that hunger and desire will be created and prophetic abilities will be imparted. When we think we have finally reached all there is to know, I believe we will be shocked at the fact that we had never even scraped the surface of what is possible for us. The Lord has in store for us things that have never even crossed the mind of man. So, this book is a combination of teachings from revelation the Lord has given me and an unveiling of dreams, visions, signs and wonders that the Lord began to give me as I learnt how to grow and function as a Seer Prophet. As you read through this book, you will receive impartation and unlocking to engage with God through experiential encounter. It is important to steward and journalize it. Daily we grow into the fullness of Christ and into our calling, which is actually a simplified version of saying 'the path of Christ' of which we are all coming into realisation and manifestation of. Wisdom records its experience in all manner of forms because revelation comes in seed form and the unfolding of that seed gives birth to new fruits and seeds therein. Always look back and see passed dreams and visions since the Kingdom builds upon itself.

At the start of 2020 the Lord guided me into writing this book and gave me the title in a dream. With each passing day the Lord brought the words to life on these pages, as I yielded to the Holy Spirit, He gave me the verbiage and terminology necessary for the spiritual gifting impartations and teachings. As I began to write on the governing authority of the Lord in later chapters, I was taken to Heaven in a vision while asleep and I came face to face with the Father. He was wrapped in thick darkness, the only way that my eyes were allowed to see Him, since His true brilliance no man can see. This same vision mirrored the thick dark cloud Moses was taken into to be with God. As I was falling through this darkness beholding the face of the Father, an explosive banner of words shot through the frame of my mind. 'I have given you governmental authority'. I awoke and cried bitterly. There were a tonne of things that the Lord showed me during this encounter but that may be revealed in future books or chapters. What did that fully mean, time will tell. But I want to allude to the expectations you need to have as you go through this book. Expect your perspective to change, expect to uncover things you have never heard of, or expect truth that you knew deep down to be revealed as well. Keep in mind that everything is to honour Holy Spirit and to give glory to Jesus and the Father. So, with whatever you agree with or disagree with, you are powerful to believe or reject because truth will reveal itself in due season.

I receive just as much understanding by giving this knowledge and my greatest takeaway is that what you frame with your mind can become your reality. You are a son of God, made to be exactly like God in every way. Make everything about Him first, for without relationship, eternal life and godliness means nothing! Now this is eternal life, that we may know Him, the only true God and Jesus Christ (John 17:3).

Let Us Pray Together Before We Start.

Father thank you for the relationship we have with You. We ask You to bring to us the seven Spirits of the Lord to begin to tutor us and give us revelation into the Kingdom arena and its functioning. Holy Spirit will You be our guide as you bring to remembrance all things that Jesus has taught us and begin to teach us all things in all of creation. Help us to know Your ways, to understand and govern the realms of existence as godlike beings manifesting as true sons of God and co-heirs with Christ. Let the Holy Spirit speak through the words in this book to teach us, direct us and activate the greater dimensions of faith and its functionality so that nothing will be too hard for us. We ask in the name of Jesus. Amen!

Now I Want To Pray For You.

Father in the name of Jesus I declare over the readers of this book, that the eyes of their understanding may be enlightened to understand the mysteries of God as prophetic people; may their hearts be transformed, and their functioning processes altered to a Heavenly capacity. I speak an impartation of love, righteousness, joy and the administration of the Kingdom of God into the words of this book so that every reader will be activated and brought into a greater depth of understanding and desire for You. Help every reader to engage with You and to realise their authority and the beauty of the relationship to that which you have called them into. May the spirit of Wisdom and Revelation be given to you to unfold the true depths of the knowledge of the love of our Lord Jesus Christ. Amen!

2

Desiring More

    There I was hanging from the edge of a mountain cliff with one hand, unable to hold myself up for much longer let alone the person below me whose life was literally in the palm of my hand. With all of my strength I held onto his wrist to save him from a gruesome fall to his death. He kicked and screamed and pleaded for his life to be saved. And then suddenly I felt a hand reach from above the cliff face and grab a hold of mine. At that moment I had no strength, but strength was imparted! I looked and I saw two men upon the mountain looking down at us. One I did not know the other was Jesus. As Jesus grabbed my hand, I felt a surge of power flood into me. Strength was ignited and with one full swing I was able to swing this dear stranger that I almost let slip past my fingers a few moments ago, up above the edge of the cliff. The unknown friend caught him and put me out of the dreadful fear of letting a man fall to his death from the palm of my hand. With loving eyes peering over the edge onto mine, I was locked, transfixed with Jesus as He pulled me up. My life was saved and so was the stranger's. I was on the top of a very high mountain, but I was not at the highest point. Here I was standing face to face with the King of Heaven and Earth Himself. There was no beard. He simply had the gentlest smile, a white robe and a golden sash. I followed Him into what seemed to be a cave with a flight of stairs. On reaching the top we now stood on the highest point overlooking a vast number of trees. Endless in sight and as green as any Christmas tree could ever be! As the four of us stood and looked at the beautiful forest of trees beneath us and into the distance, I for some reason stumbled and fell backwards onto a teleportation platform. I was translated in a mere second onto another mountain. I was changed and so were my clothes. I had a robe on, and I held a staff in my right hand. As I walked a few steps up this mountain pathway I stood once again overlooking an endless array of trees, but this time I was alone.

I had awoken from an intense dream, one that would forever setup the rest of my life. I believe much of what the dream reveals is yet to come to pass or surface, however it marked me that day and put a burning hunger inside of me, one that cannot be quenched until I see it to fruition.

At the time I was still 20 years old, a few months away from my 21st birthday. I remember distinctly what a rebellious son I was professing Jesus but didn't truly know Him. I knew about Him, I read the scriptures, so I thought I knew Him. But I didn't know Him enough to act anything like Him or had a heart like His to represent Him. I'd venture to say that we will never stop learning to know Him more and more for all of eternity. Could you believe that I was even baptised with the Holy Spirit, speaking in tongues and yet still living like hell. This is what happens when you are told about God, read the Bible as a religious book, even met God, but never taken the time to cultivate a relationship beyond the scriptures with the one true God. God first in your life means that He is at the forefront of every decision, action, motive, character, every thought and every word that comes out of our mouth, but religion has a funny way of putting you through the motions and allowing you to think you know God or are getting His blessing because we read the Bible or attend a church service once a week. The measure that we know God is directly proportional to the extent that we love as well as personify it.

'Whoever does not love does not know God, because God is love'. (1 John 4:8 NIV)

The willingness to transform ourselves into love when made aware of sin in our lives, comes from humility and that is only obtained by the Fear of the Lord. So that is where I needed to start by the Fear of God and separating myself unto holiness, which meant not having the same goals or caring for the things the world cares for.

Before this dream happened, I had come to a point of my life where my character was completely flawed. It was at its worst. I thought it was the people around me and so automatically I blamed them, but I came to the end of myself very quickly. I locked myself in my room and cried out to God on my bedroom floor. I asked God, 'is it me or is it them?' And with a loving fatherly voice, without any condemnation I simply heard, 'it is you'. At the same time the thoughts of God dropped into my Spirit, it was simple yet so profound. 'How they act is not your concern, but how you act in retaliation is your concern even if they are wrong and you are right. Your job is only to love'. My life changed. A few simple words from God and my life was to be put to death so that Christ may live through me. From making it all about me, I made it all about Jesus so much so that I could think about nothing else. Did life change overnight? No, but it felt like everything I did apart from doing all I could to be a friend of God was meaningless. I finally took it seriously, I didn't just incorporate Jesus into life, it was Jesus and then do life. I listened to every sermon I could on righteousness, so that I could do right in His eyes, not my own.

'There is a way that seems right to a man, but its end is the way of death'. (Proverbs 14:12 NKJV)

I downloaded the bible audiobook and I began listening to it continuously over and over. And at the same time, I took praying in tongues to another level. In one day, my tongues grew from one sentence to a stream of sentences. I was so desperate to know God and live for God that I decided to listen to the audio bible on my headphones even while working and praying in tongues at the same time. Within two days of doing this without stopping, (I don't think I even stopped for an hour), I was given this dream. Was it because I prayed so diligently that I was given such an incredible and breathtaking dream, no I believe it was the desperate hunger and the groans that I could not utter with my voice that allowed Holy Spirit to speak on my behalf and call forth what was written on my destiny scroll in Heaven. I'm sure that many people have had much greater experiences, visitations and much more but for me this was the first and one true thing that put hope for a godly future into me. Without it I wouldn't have such a deep desire to know God or be called into ministry. I had much greater experiences being slain in the Spirit and vibrating on my bed for 3 days in the presence of God, crying bucket loads in the presence of God but none of those experiences changed my heart's desire until I saw His face and encountered Him alone. It was not in a church meeting or being told to experience Him by someone else, but it was of my own will and my desperate pursuit of Him. From then onwards I continued to seek the Lord with all my heart.

'You will seek me and find me when you seek me with all your heart.' (Jeremiah 29: 13 NIV)

Back to the dream on the mountain with God, I had woken with the thoughts *Mark 4:27-29* as if I had been keeping my mind focused on that verse for a long time. Hurriedly in that awoken drunken stupor, I scrambled for my bible on my bed next to me.

'Night and day, he sleeps and wakes, and the seed sprouts and grows, though he knows not how. All by itself the Earth produces a crop— first the stalk, then the head, then grain that ripens within.

And as soon as the grain is ripe, he swings the sickle, because the harvest has come.' (Mark 4:27-29 NKJV)

I believe the Lord had shown me the end times harvest of souls, with the trees being the multitude of people. Was I called to be a mass harvester or a person to lead in an area or be a voice for Christ in the end time generation? Only time will tell. Several questions flowed through my mind. Was I meant to do something now? How do I have more dreams like this and get revelation on them? I had tonnes of questions, but I needed the Spirit of wisdom and revelation. At this time, I did not know anything about the prophetic all I wanted was to know God. Days passed and I needed a confirmation that it really was Jesus on the mountain that I saw. Even though I had the knowing in my Spirit I just needed to know if this was just some random dream or not. Strangely enough, He didn't have a beard but yet I knew it was Jesus. As I was sitting at my computer at work still thinking about the dream, I suddenly noticed in my mind a verse that seemed to have been lingering there, as if I've always known the verse. The overwhelming thoughts were 'they pulled my beard, Isaiah 50'. I looked it up unsurprised, instead I felt relieved. *Isaiah 50:6 NKJV says, 'I gave my back to those who struck Me, and My cheeks to those who plucked out the beard; I did not hide My face from shame and spitting'.* It was Him and I was learning the language of the Spirit. I was hearing God's voice in my thoughts and literally in my chest cavity, in my heart.

Since that time the Lord began to birth the prophetic in me, but I never knew it was called the prophetic. All I was doing was trying to be with Jesus when no one was looking. Here are some of the things that began happening when I began stewarding the dreams. One after the other more came, and much more often. I valued the gift, so it increased like a well-trained muscle. I spoke in tongues all the time when I was not speaking to someone else or to God in English. The dreams became clearer and I could remember it as if it were clearer than an actual memory. Revelation and teaching dreams came more often where I was taught by Saints, some still alive and some who have gone on to be with Jesus. I was even taught with Jesus Himself on spiritual matters such as learning to wait on God, fasting, deliverance, the secret place and more. I began seeing angels in dreams and recognising warning dreams of actions that I should take and especially what I should not do. I began waking at odd hours of the night to pray for key events that were to take place even in the political arena which I don't normally follow. Signs and wonders began happening. Words of knowledge for people began appearing in my mind as a picture. Some I understood immediately, others I did not. I was just starting to learn what these things meant and how I should steward it. I was not in control of it, but this was clearly only the beginning.

Since that time nothing happened in the natural in terms of goals or dream fulfilment that God placed in my heart. In fact, it was quite the opposite, every friend I made was gone out of sight, every job opportunity came to an abrupt end as if I was meant to leave a mark and disappear, my extended family began to notice I was unmovable about Jesus and with it came remarks that I couldn't avoid. Not every persecution is physical and the ones doing it, Christian and non-Christian, friends, family and acquaintances didn't even know they were doing it, but the Lord always trained me and reminded me that my job was to love and to never show any scars. But that's easier said than done, but the faster I forgave, the faster I grew in intimacy with God. Nothing internally stopped me. Over time I grew in relationship with the Lord, I prayed for people and some got healed, the majority didn't. I'm sure I looked like a complete fool. But that's ok I was learning how to hear from God, gaining boldness and learning to love. Regardless of me pursuing God all I had were dreams, the word of God and any sermons I could find. However, I did discover that certain family members did secretly have a very powerful relationship with the Lord, but I had never noticed it since I hardly ever saw them being in other countries. There were no friends who had any form of relationship with God that I did, even church friends were so into the motions of religion and not the deep truths of the Spirit and the power of God that I was put off. Even the

Christian friends I thought that had deeper relationships with God had changed churches. In my world sphere I seemed to be the only person around that seemed to be enjoying the manifest presence of God and going deeper into the things of the Spirit. I realised quickly even many of the Christian people I knew from church just incorporated Jesus but never lived to the point of reckless abandon or desired to become love. I never met anyone led by the Spirit or missionaries who got over excited about seeing miracles, healing, prophetic utterances, dreams, signs and wonders or anything else. It felt like the Jesus I was beginning to know was more real and was exactly how the word of God portrayed Him to be. Truly the scriptures speak of Him, but they refused to come to Him (John 5:39-40), they just wanted to play church, sing a few songs and listen to a feel-good message rather than be the church, a beautiful bride of Christ without spot or blemish. We ought to be the hands and feet of Jesus. Even the missions work that I saw happening didn't have any stories of healings, deliverances, and definitely not dead raising. They were just building homes and giving food. There is a place for that, but even non-Christ followers do that, so what was the real difference? It seemed to be a trunkless elephant, a church that had no power and barely taught deeper truths of the Word. So, I left church for a time in pursuit of the power of God and His heart by myself in my bedroom until God told me to go back to a church.

In my stage of isolation from church I had learnt to wait on God, getting up at 3am to pray and seek the Lord, however I did not remain as consistent as I could have in the 4th watchmen hours of the night, but the Lord was calling me to wait on Him more consistently, everyday aiming to spend as long as necessary to feel satisfied and full inside, no matter how many hours a day it took in worship and waiting on God. And what came out of it was intimacy and relationship followed by the most ridiculous amount of dreams, signs and wonders that began showing up. Where did they come from and what was so different this time around? I don't believe it was simply seeking God that did it. It wasn't the 3am meetings with God on my bedroom floor. It was true intimacy, desiring nothing greater than I did God. Learning to hear what God wanted me to do and acting accordingly became all I lived for. We should know that prayer is not simply a one-sided pursuit of God. Prayer is your 'amen' (so let it be) to God's 'Yes'. It is in fact a relationship, a two-way transaction. Not only was I pursuing God, but I found out very quickly that He had been pursuing me all along and the more faithful I became by spending time in a consistent manner according to the way that He desired it, the more I began to see my life unfold. I lost mine. I found His.

God told me to go back to church, a very different church which I thought had even less of the real person of Jesus. I was wrong. Within a few months of going to the church it was clear why God spoke clearly to go to this church. It was as if Heaven broke out and angelic assistance was sent out to push me into destiny and bring me friends who talked about Jesus all day, every day! It wasn't in the church but in the bible study groups that the Lord led me to that truly changed my life. Not only were they singing in tongues, they were slain in the Spirit, drunk on the Spirit, people were falling out in the Spirit, there were prophecies unleashed, there were signs and wonders showing up and even demons were being cast out. And no one knew them. They were hidden ones dedicated to ministry works of the Lord. Heaven invaded my space. Signs, wonders, manifestations, baptisms of fire and the prophetic broke out. Hearing the voice of God and seeing in the Spirit became commonplace and seeing dreams and visions only increased! It wasn't just me alone in my bedroom anymore with God. God answered my prayer and I found people on the same road as me, that would set me up for destiny.

It was, is and shall forever will be an honour to serve God with the prophetic. The most exciting life is one that stewards the voice of God for yourself and for God's people. And the Lord has blessed me to impart the same anointing and gifts to others, so that is what will be done as you read this book and go through the prayer activations and practice tasks. Please do not skip to the activations without reading through the book since I would like you to have a firm foundation to understand what you will begin to experience in the realms of the Spirit. This book is to bring glory to God by activating His children in the prophetic so all may operate in the prophetic and in the power of the Spirit for the coming latter rain movement.

Activation

Tonight, as you go to sleep spend time praying in tongues and turning your attention to Jesus. Leave worship music or even godly soaking music in the background as you fall asleep.

Prayer

Lord make Yourself the desire of my heart, that I may grow in relationship with You and live the life that You have called me to. Show me my giftings and how to grow them that I may be a blessing to others. Amen!

3

Levels Of Intimacy And Relationship

Who Are You To God?

In every dispensation there has been a greater revelation released of who we are. The reason for this is because the body of Christ is growing into maturity and so the extent to which we can handle the revelation as a collective body, is the revelation released by God. However, your personal revelation could be lesser or greater than the understanding during that dispensation. Of course, we as prophetic people, desiring more of God, would always want greater understanding of our identity so that we can walk and operate at a greater level. In saying that, we should also be patient with those who cannot yet handle the revelation and the wisdom that proceeds from that understanding. Understanding who you are will allow you to operate in a greater dimension, with more ease and accuracy. But at the same time, we need to understand that with it comes a greater responsibility and greater level of accountability to God.

The butter knife analogy. You wouldn't give a sharp knife to a child, since they could hurt themselves. In a manner of speaking, they are not yet responsible enough to use the knife because they don't know what it is for and can cause more harm than good. Likewise, you also need to spend time with the child to teach what the knife is for and the different types of knives. For example, a butcher knife is different to a bread knife and a butter knife. The uses are all different and the shapes as well. Even though it appears to be just a knife it is important to know which knife to use depending on the food. Likewise, we as prophetic people start off as butter knives, the shapes and sizes being the different types of prophetic abilities such as dreams, words of knowledge, prophesying etc. But we should never remain as a small butter knife with its capabilities, we ought to recognise the double-edged knife we carry! That of course being the Sword of the Spirit, which is the word of God (Hebrews 4:12) and we should aim to become as sharp as possible so that we can be of greater benefit to all.

In the fallen way of life, the more knowledge you have the more you are qualified to do. This can be likened to eating from the Tree of the Knowledge of Good and Evil. For example, obtaining a Master's degree would qualify you for a higher paying job and all you need to do is apply and hope you get it. But in the realms of the Spirit what qualifies you for operating from greater revelatory realms is your passionate pursuit of intimacy with God. This can be likened to eating from the Tree of Life. We have all been given salvation through Jesus Christ as a free gift and have become children of God. But operating from a greater revelatory realm has a price tag and the price is the level of intimacy you are willing to have with Holy Spirit, since He is the one that teaches you how to use the sword. Relationship is the key!

We are adopted already as sons of God (Ephesians 1:5); we are friends of God if we do what He commands us (John 15:14) and we as the church are the future bride of Christ (Revelation 22:17). However, to operate from the realms of a friend, son or bride requires different levels of intimacy. As the knives have different levels of sharpness from a butter knife, to a bread knife, to a butcher knife so do the spiritual realms of glory or levels of intimacy, going from friend to son, to bride. We also see this in operation, and these correspond in like manner that we move from faith, to hope, to love. The greatest of these is love. These will directly affect your revelation of who you are and your operations in the prophetic. In the great love chapters we see that all may prophesy as Paul explains in *1 Corinthians 14:1 (NKJV) 'Pursue love and desire spiritual gifts, but especially that you may prophesy'*. No one starts off with a perfect gift but through practise it is trained just like any skill in the natural. We see this in:

1 Corinthians 13:9 (NKJV) 'For we know in part and we prophesy in part, but when that which is perfect has come, then that which is in part will be done away with.'

In light of this, I have noticed through prophesying to others over time that as you grow in your level of intimacy with God and your love for others, your prophetic gifting increases in all dimensions, whether it is through stewarding dreams, prophetic utterances, songs, words of knowledge, words of wisdom or even signs and wonders. With this being said if you operate out of a friendship realm your prophetic abilities will be limited to only hearing from the Spirit at that level, the same with the sonship realm and greater still from the bridal realm. So, your revelation of knowing who you are determines these factors. I like to think of it like this, since I am always eager to grow in the prophetic as I'm sure you are. A husband should be able to share anything with his wife since there is the greatest level of trust and the wife's ability to become one through intimate union; and a son should be a complete shadow of his father knowing and growing into all that his father is and a friend whom God confides in before executing an action. Finally, there is also the servant realm whom have the greatest humility. However, we should all be operating from a bondservant realm as Jesus did but also the above relationship realms. If you have heard these terms before, your understanding and revelation of them may be different, they are not necessarily wrong because we all should be able to grow in our own relationship and understandings with God and add to one another's understanding to grow in greater relationship with the Lord. God actually desires you to operate at a higher awareness of who you are but if you cannot fulfill the accountability and responsibility process, you will squander the dominion, authority and the higher spiritual giftings by letting pride in. God will bring every deed into judgement even though people already judge a leader's integrity by default. Was it self-serving or was it God serving? Did it come from intimacy or a different mindset? And rightfully so, we wouldn't want a wolf in sheep's clothing leading us into a pit. Likewise, the Lord withholds until character and integrity is developed at the right capacity to walk in the greater level of revelation and authority. As a son your responsibility and accountability is aimed to be as great as your Heavenly Father's since you are an ambassador going about His business. As a friend we are entrusted to reliability and like-mindedness. For a wife to a husband there comes a greater faithfulness, responsibility, accountability and intimacy where although all that is His is hers, the Lord acts on the process of Ephesians 5:25 - *'Husbands, love your wives, just as Christ loved the church and gave Himself up for her...'*. To the level of which realm you have nurtured and sustained, so are you allowed to walk in. Even though you fall into all categories, your revelation of them manifests them in your prophetic abilities as well as your life in general. We may at times see a leader with an exceptional gifting who operates from that gifting instead of operating from a greater revelation and the necessary character. He would be putting himself in a bad position only for many to see him fall in the public eyes due to hidden sins. This has happened for truly greatly anointed people. Every deed good or bad is brought into the light. So, intimacy with God should always be the first priority in your ministry. Before every meeting personally give God glory as well as after every meeting, and secretly give God the glory because we are merely carriers of His glory and pride can easily sneak in when the carnal nature is not killed off.

Royalty

You are not ordinary. You are royalty!

'For as he thinks in his heart, so is he... 'Proverbs 23:7 (NKJV)

There was once a prince who had just taken over His father's position who had passed away. Some people had said that they should kill him as well. But they were stopped by others who said he was too young, and he would go to Heaven and that would be too good of a thing for his evil father. So, they sent him to a witch to learn how to curse and become evil so when he dies, he would go to hell. The witch tried everything she could to make him repeat those words, but the boy would not. And the witch screamed and asked why won't you say it? He replied, 'I was born to be a prince!'. When you are royalty and you know it, you don't just act like everyone else. The way you speak is different, you have authority that others do not, you dress differently and it's because you are! Is that a proud thing? Surely not, it is a humbling truth to realise that you have been tasked with dominion-ship over the Earth as a royal king and priest from Heaven.

Obtaining revelation of your kingship and priesthood allows you to operate from greater realms still. It is an honour to consider this and hard to come to terms with, but *Revelation 1:6 says 'To Him who loved us and washed us from our sins in His own blood and has made us kings and priests to His God and Father, to Him be glory and dominion forever and ever. Amen.'*

As prophetic people, it is important to realise that what you decree and declare or even speak by happenstance manifests and can even become a law. Jesus gave us the keys to the Kingdom in:

Matthew 16:19 (NIV) 'I will give you the keys of the Kingdom of Heaven;

whatever you bind on Earth will be bound in Heaven, and whatever you loose on Earth will be loosed in Heaven."

If a person is allowed to operate with such authority, if He were not guided by the Holy Spirit, He would wreck his world. And so, we already do see that happen in many people's lives by the choices they make and the actions they take due to selfishness rather than the heart of God. You do not need the Holy Spirit to act as a king and you do not need the Holy Spirit to act as a priest either. We see this throughout the religious and secular world. However, it is worse still if we act on our own accord without the Holy Spirit and delve into the prophetic. The only difference between a psychic and a prophet is the influence of the Spirit they are operating from. Prophets of God operate out of the voice, power and functioning of the Holy Spirit but any other medium or psychics operate out of demonic spirits and their power. Therefore, intimacy with Holy Spirit is vital and love is always the goal. Even a child is known by his conduct and the things they let out of their mouth. They require discipline either from a parent or Holy Spirit. But as adults we are judged by people in a greater capacity since we are supposed to have a reign on our tongue. With age is meant to come maturity but this is not the case. It is pointed out that the power of life and death is in your tongue in *Proverbs 18:21*. It is no wonder that we create immeasurable influence by our choice of words. It goes beyond this when we understand that as kings, priests and sons of God with God living inside of our body, that we should be paying close attention to what we say in our day to day conversations, minor and especially major agreements and disagreements. It's clear that we are royalty, priests and sons of God. We can operate out of different realms due to our level of revelation and intimacy of our positions as sons, friends or brides of Christ, as well as a king and priest. However, what we are, is yet to be discovered in as much revelation.

What Are We?

We are gods! This is a very sensitive topic that many people are not ready for. But I am trusting that since this book is in your hands then you want to know the whole truth and nothing but the truth, no matter how hard it may be to digest.

John 10:34 (NIV) 'Jesus answered them, 'Is it not written in your Law, I said "You are gods"?'

We see here that *Psalms 82:6* is quoted by Jesus explaining to the Jews who were in the middle of stoning Him because blindly they thought he was blaspheming, when in actuality Jesus was revealing the truth. Jesus was not only showing us that He was the Son of God, but He was calling us into a realisation of who and what we actually are that God intended us to be when He created us. We should all know that we are a spirit as God is a spirit, we live inside a body and we have a soul. As prophetic people we need to grow in our understanding of each of these dimensions since we are made in the image of God. Each of these beings of existence has a language of its own. The more you train it, the louder it becomes.

The Spirit is you, the soul is your operating centre like a computer CPU and the body you have on Earth is portal device with gateways that allow you to operate in the physical plane. We have other bodies, a spiritual body in Heaven, a resurrected glorified body which is to come and others that will be revealed (1 Corinthians 15).

Language of the Spirit

The language of the Spirit is 'knowing'. This is who you are and what you really are, a spirit-being. Inside of your Spirit you have gateways.

They mirror your physical senses, however they are in fact more real than your body and are your true senses. Ever had a gut feeling something wasn't right with a circumstance, a decision or a certain somebody? You are not trying to play judge, it is just what was observed in your spirit about that thing. You felt uneasy or you just didn't feel 'right', and that is because if you have a close relationship with God, that is in fact Holy Spirit talking to your spirit to give you insider knowledge. However, if you are carnally minded then you will judge externally rather than discerning by the voice of the Spirit which as I said is 'knowing'. Many others have called this 'impressions' or an inner witness. When you hear in the Spirit it can at times be audible. Have you ever felt like someone called your name? But when you checked to see who called you, there wasn't anyone who did? This can be an angel or the voice of God trying to get your attention. Many nights I have awoken to my name being called in the middle of the night and I knew by the Spirit that it was Father God. I've noticed that this happens when God requires me to get up and pray usually around 3am which is the fourth watch hour. The funny thing is, it always sounds like my dad is calling me when this has happened. We see this with Samuel thinking that Eli was calling him in 1 Samuel 3. There are different levels of hearing in the Spirit. As you grow in intimacy with the Lord and spend more time with Him your senses grow and you become familiar with what hearing in the spirit feels and sounds like, however they do vary according to the situation of which the Lord is trying to get a message across to you. It may come in dreams, in prayer or even randomly living day to day.

In January 2019, with a team of incredibly anointed individuals, we held our first crusade under the name 'The Gift Crusade'. Whilst in Cape Town a woman approached me after a prophetic worship session that I led. She told me that she had a dream with no pictures, but all she heard was my name Kurshin. She woke up and thought it was a very strange name, she had never heard it before. It is of course a very unique name that my parents told me that they made up. The lady typed my name into google and it just so happened to be the correct spelling as well, which in itself feels like a miracle to me! A video of the radio interview we had at CCFM 107.5 came up where we announced the crusade that was happening a few days later. She told me that is how she knew God told her to come to the crusade. Amazing! She had an inner knowing of what she was to do. If God is trying to get your attention, it will be loud and clear! So always be curious regarding the things of God and you may just end up on the road of destiny.

Well that's for hearing but what about seeing in the Spirit. You may get dreams or visions to perceive the voice of the Lord. It states within Habakkuk 2:1 '...I will look to see what he will say to me...'. Unfortunately, if you were like me and you grew up with people saying things like 'it was just a dream' and you stopped getting dreams, it is because you have unconsciously shut down your ability to see dreams. Simply repent and apply the blood of Christ over any strongholds and it will come back as you pursue the Lord. We will speak on pulling down strongholds later on in the book and I will give you clear steps on how the Lord taught me how to do this. Often, you'll find little children complaining that there is a monster under his bed or hiding in the cupboard. Usually this is followed by the child being scared and parents saying there's nothing there. The problem with that, is that little children have not yet been desensitised to seeing in the spirit and so they are actually seeing or perceiving something in the spirit realm. Parents have unknowingly shut down the ability for the child to perceive in the Spirit by forcing them to believe nothing was there instead of handling it as demonic spirits of fear. It takes a lot of work to undo the trauma of desensitisation in later years. This also applies to your imagination which is also known as your mind's eye or the eyes of your heart/spirit. Please be careful with reading or seeing anything on the 'third eye' which is a name given by the occult and secular world. It is important to realise that the imagination is not fake.

Matthew 5:28 NKJV says *'But I say to you that whoever looks at a woman to lust for her has already committed adultery with her in his heart.'*

This word heart refers to imagination where dreams or closed visions happen not merely a place of desire. You actually think with your heart, your brain is only the processing centre. When children have imaginary friends, we should consider asking the Lord about it and trying to see what they see, or we will fall into the trap of closing their eyes to the spiritual realm because of ignorance. There are many angelic hosts that can interact with us, however we need to be open. Pursuing the Lord in relationship will help us discern Spirits from the Lord and those that are not. We also have the responsibility to protect our children from demons masquerading as angels of light. Test the spirits by getting them to confess whether they have come in the name of Jesus as well as praying for the discernment of Spirits.

One night I had awoken acutely aware that satan had come to check on who I was. I couldn't see him with my physical eyes but in the realm of the spirit you can see in any direction. I knew in the spirit that this was the case and that the Lord allowed me to see this and to have no fear at all. I can still remember it and I always wondered why that took place. This was about 5 years before I had any form of ministry, of course no one would believe me but now that I am being used for the Lord's work I understand why. It is important to remember to take everything before the Lord in prayer. Building a strong relationship as a Seer Prophet requires you to often see into the Kingdom realm, so maintain the fear of God in you, and reject any spirits of fear or the fear of man which is demonic.

Onto smelling in the Spirit (1 Corinthians 12:17). During a prayer session I could smell Anzac biscuits and it was so strong it felt like it was freshly baked, and someone was waving it under my nose. I had no idea why I was smelling it until one of my friends pointed out that one of the ladies had just spoken at an Anzac Day meeting and was able to share her faith. I was also told later that it also could have been for someone else whose relative served in the Anzac war. I don't know anything about the Anzac war, but the Lord allowed me to sense something by the Spirit to encourage these two people. The Lord cares about the things you care about, even more so than you do. It's always about love. If we pursue love, God can use you in any way for His glory.

On another occasion I could smell flowers while praying over a friend and I knew immediately that the Lord was releasing a new fragrance for them to carry, meaning that they would leave new impressions on people that they met. This seemed so simple but was quite an important one since our walks with God can sometimes require that we have influence over others as leaders. The Lord often requires us as prophets to speak or decree a new thing to replace the old season.

Moving on to tasting in the Spirit. Psalm 34:8 NIV says - *'Taste and see that the Lord is good; blessed is the one who takes refuge in him.'* At times in situations where I had felt uncomfortable in, I would get this bitter taste in my mouth and I didn't recognise it as anything until I tasted sweetness in my mouth during an event, that I knew the Lord wanted me to attend. This sense of taste can also be given revelation to by the Hebraic mindset pertaining to experiential knowledge. This form of experiencing the goodness of the Lord in difficult situations is also how the Lord draws us into intimacy with Him. However, according to the Greek mindset and in the realm of the spirit this can actually turn up as real taste similar to the other senses. On other occasions I have been made acutely aware of the horrible taste and smell of different evil spirits manifesting in other people's bodies but at the same time a fresh, clean taste and smell in the atmosphere at events where the Spirit of the Lord was present. This often happens at conferences that have been prayed diligently over for months prior and so the arenas are saturated with the presence of God (Ezekiel 36:25).

Finally, onto the sense of touch. Feelings are one of the most heightened senses in the realm of the Spirit. From getting words of knowledge by experiencing a pain in the same part of the body as the sick person to feeling the heavy weight of the Kavod glory of the Lord. We often see this when people fall over from the anointing, but it can be as intense as not being able to breath as in the case with services that were led by a powerful evangelist by the name of Smith Wigglesworth and greater still where the body becomes so heavy that you can barely move. This has happened to me many times where I could not move, or I vibrated as if being electrocuted. On two occasions I had to be dragged out of the church because I became too heavy from the glory. Just to give you a perspective I only weighed around 55kg, but the presence of God was felt so heavy on my Spirit that two six-foot men could barely lift me, almost dragging me from the ground. This is partially my fault I told God either You kill me or give me everything I need to be used for Your glory. I'll tell you more about what came out of such an experience in later chapters. Experiences of the power of God like that mark you and change your life forever. It is important to recognise that dreams do not only come with seeing and hearing. You can also smell, taste and feel as well. In certain dreams I have fought with robbers and woke up with my hands sore for the rest of the day with internal pain like muscle soreness. In another dream I was swimming in an ocean in Heaven treading water, jumping into other people's boats and I had awoken with my thigh muscles extremely sore as if I actually was swimming for a long time. By telling you of these dreams, visions and sensory abilities you will first gain understanding to recognise it when it happens to you and secondly impartation. When you begin experiencing the same, you will be able to draw on like experiences to have a grid for what you are experiencing.

Everyone's experience is different; however, everyone has the same abilities to perceive by all senses in the Spirit. We should keep an open mind to let the Lord lead us and for Holy Spirit to take us deeper. Never try to engage the spirit realm without entering through the door which is Christ Jesus himself. Without entering through Jesus, you are open to attacks from the enemy and demons can enter into your body and can cripple you or cause problems for you in the natural, whether physically, mentally or emotionally. This is why people who have opened their chakras by the use of weed, drugs or engaging in eastern philosophical practices such as yoga can leave them in a broken state, often cognitively affected or tormented by demons. Jesus is the way, the truth and the life, you go to the Father through Him (John 14:6) He is also the gate or the door that you should enter the spirit or the Kingdom of Heaven by (John 10:9-16). This is among the reasons why Jesus will normally initiate an encounter in the Spirit first in case we get it wrong. But we are able to enter His gates by thanksgiving and praise (Psalm 100:4) if we learn to diligently pursue Him in relationship. It is an important time for the church to wake up to the realities of the things of the Spirit and gain a handle on it because there are great deceptions and witchcraft at play.

For we do not wrestle against flesh and blood, but against principalities, against powers, against the rulers of darkness of this age, against spiritual hosts of wickedness in the Heavenly places (Ephesians 6:12 NKJV).

Never engage the enemy without first knowing your authority in Christ, instead we should use spiritual experiences as a means to get closer to God and become one with Him.

Activation

Write down every characteristic that Jesus has in your journal or frame it on your walls! And then begin to declare that as Jesus is so are you right now. The more you do this, the more your mind will be renewed, and your belief system will change to allow you to realise that you were made by God for God to operate the way He does. The goal is always to operate from the bridal realm, however not everyone is willing to put in the time to nurture such a relationship. If you desire it, you can be a part of it. Begin by putting aside time everyday to be with Jesus and ask the Lord to draw you closer to His heart. Also ask the Lord to begin to show you the best method for yourself to hear His voice by the language of the Spirit so that you will not miss His voice.

Prayer

Lord I pray for ears to hear, eyes to see and an understanding heart that I may know your perfect will and act accordingly for my life. I also pray for great discernment to be able to test the spirits. Fill me with every bit of power that You have in store for my life and begin to use me as your vessel. Increase my receptivity to the things of the spirit and may I never neglect the development of my relationship with You. May I walk in the completeness of my identity in You and may my life begin to bring glory to Your name. In Jesus name, Amen!

4

A Prophet's Authority

The concept of authority is one that must be grasped and practiced for us to grow as Seer Prophets. The reason why it is such a fundamental principle is because even though all people are designed to see into the spirit realm, not everyone is designed to be a Seer Prophet. Let me explain. Being a prophet is not a title, it is a function, or a role given to you by God for the betterment of the church, His Ecclesia which is actually the church government of God on the Earth. This of course pertains to the office of a prophet and not merely prophetic people. All people baptised with the Holy Spirit should be prophetic because the Holy Spirit living inside of us teaches us all things (1 John 2:27). Prophetic means being able to understand and perceive the insights and revelatory knowledge of God and not only predictions of the future. All men can see visions and dreams, whether they are sealed by the Holy Spirit or not. However, the message that comes from dreams and visions are rarely interpreted by one who does not have eyes to see, ears to hear or have a heart to understand God's message. The world may try to interpret by natural reasoning but without a relationship with the one who gave the dream to explain the dream, all it surmounts to is guessing what it may mean.

There are different types of prophets such as those who see (*Hozeh*) into the realm of the spirit specific pictures or hear in the spirit specific words. Most often it is for other people. There are seers that reveal secret mysterious for the future from God (*Roeh*) to the church. There are also prophets who bubble over with the infilling of the Holy Spirit to give prophetic utterances (*Nabi*), proclamations, or prophetic songs about what the Lord is doing. Prophet Kim Clement is an example of a *Nabi*, Prophet Bob Jones was an example of a *Roeh* and often you may see prophets prophesying over people in the church calling out names and places with an encouraging word specifically for their life which are the *Hozeh*. Most often *Roeh* prophets are followed frequently by signs, wonders and the angelic, although this may happen occasionally for any children of God to give guidance for their life. Each prophet perceives differently but it is generally for the edification of the church or others. All children of God can access all areas of giftings, however the major gift that comes naturally or by default out from you is the function that the Lord has chosen for you as the primary medium.

As a prophet you are required to be a messenger for the Lord and carry His messages to the church and to others. The spirit of prophecy is also the testimony of Jesus, therefore we ought to recognise that as a prophet the authority placed on our shoulders pertains to the Government of Heaven (Isaiah 9:6) and the words of governing, through representing Christ as a Heavenly ambassador. You are physically, mentally, emotionally and spiritually designed to pick up on the wavelengths of what Heaven is doing and decree it into existence into the Earth realm. Therefore, as the one hearing, seeing and perceiving by all of your senses what Heaven is doing for a person, church, a city, region or country, you have a moral obligation to intercede/pray into it and see that the will of God is accomplished. Saint Augustine stated, 'Without God, man cannot, and without man, God will not.' The Lord has specifically chosen prophets to have a forerunner type of relationship with Him and to be given insight into what He is about to accomplish on the Earth and so we as His instruments of righteousness and vessels of His glory, are required to speak out what He is doing.

'Surely the Sovereign LORD does nothing without revealing his plan to his servants the prophets' (Amos 3:7 NIV).

This is why during times where the presence of God is tangible in praise and worship services, as we enter into the high praises of the Lord, we can decree what we see in the spirit and it happens with ease. This may be the direction for the meeting or manifestations of the Glory of God. As one who has been given messages by God for others you have the obligation to speak it forth, therefore with it comes the right and the authority to do so (Deuteronomy 29:29), unless the Lord has directed you to keep certain things as secrets. Since we as prophets and prophetic people are given such insights, we should also be careful to hold our tongue when necessary and not cast our pearls before swine who don't care for the things of the prophetic or the greater things of God. People's opinions do not change the truths of God, but it can cause problems for you that can be easily avoided. Consider, are any prophetic words or insights that you know from God, necessary for that person to know for the sake of their salvation and wholeness? If it is, express it with love, but seek Holy Spirit on the right timing and manner in which it should be conveyed. If it is not necessary, then we ought to hold our tongue and let truth reveal itself in due time.

Your authority comes from the Lord. As a chosen instrument in the hand of the Lord you are no different as an ambassador of a country speaking on behalf of a country whilst overseas. Your Kingdom, Heaven, backs you in every way and you are judged by your Kingdom's laws and not the laws of the Earth. This does not mean you do not keep the laws of your state or the lands you need to travel to. The laws of Heaven are purer and more righteous than any Earthly government. And being a citizen of Heaven comes with many perks and benefits. We do not see the citizens of a Kingdom going to war but instead we see its army go to war. This is the same with the Kingdom of Heaven that releases angelic hosts to move on your behalf as you pray, decree and declare the wonderful works of the Lord into the Earth. Praying in tongues is essential since we do not always know how to pray about these things. Knowing this as a prophet gives you a greater advantage as you are required to pray into matters that you can see in the spiritual realm even though you may not have the words to adequately describe it. So, having a close relationship with the Lord is of utmost importance since the closer you are to the Chief General of the army the greater level of authority you have and the greater level of protection you have as well. And of course, that applies to everyone.

I used to struggle with the idea of authority. I always listened and obeyed my parents to the best of my abilities and my teachers in school. The problem with that is if you do not know the Lord and make sure that His voice in your life is number one, then anyone else's voice in your life becomes your God. What you submit to becomes your God. So, in the past when teachers said belittling statements, it left a mark on my identity until I took it before God and spoke His word and focused on what He said about me. His authority is greater and what He says goes. That does not mean that we do not honour and respect our parents or authorities since the bible is clear that we should respect our parents and authorities, unless it defies God's word. So, if He says, 'I am righteous by the blood of Jesus and forgiven, then I am', and if He says, 'I have been made perfect, then in His eyes I am'. We need to come into agreement with what He says or else we make ourselves our own god by holding onto our false beliefs. When Jesus called the disciples to Himself and gave them power to drive out demons and to heal the sick, it was because God gave them the authority to do so (Mark 3:13-15). You may have the power to do something, but even a thief has power to break into a house. If you own the house on the other hand you have the authority to kick that thief out. So, gaining authority from God means you have authority over all powers of the enemy. Therefore, you have all authority in Heaven and Earth as Jesus has said you do. By calling us to be one with Him, to partake in divine communion with Him, all that is His is ours, including the authority (Matthew 28:18-20). Having such power and authority can be dangerous to a prophet or any man. Since prophets are required to speak on behalf of God and influence others, developing a righteous character and relationship with God means everything because of it. God does not promote you into a level of influence because of how gifted you are with your prophetic ability but instead how purified your character and motives have become and your relationship with the Holy Spirit. We see that even Jesus had to pass certain tests in the wilderness before coming out with the power of the Holy Spirit (Luke 4:14). If the son of God was required to do so, how much more so us.

This ties in with the realisation that not anyone can invoke the name of Jesus to cast out demons or heal the sick. When we cast out demons or heal the sick in the name of Jesus, it is not synonymous to a magic word, it is the positional authority and right that you have as a son of God. This authority is greater still, since we will judge angels in the ages to come. Do we really know who or what we are? Much is to be revealed. Acts 19:11-20 speaks of the seven sons of Sceva who tried to invoke the name of Jesus to help another person, however they got badly beaten up by the demons. Why was this the case? Because they did not nurture a relationship with the Lord to be able to exercise that authority. Have you ever seen a young child that no one knew of from the street get up in front of a country's army to lead them? However, I have seen sons of CEOs of companies inherit responsibility and the employees are expected to submit to that authority as if it was the original CEO giving the orders. So, the seven sons of Sceva actually had no right to try and cast out the demons in the name of Jesus because no authority had been given to them by Jesus, having not been recognised as sons of God. As Seer Prophets we will often sense demons and see what others cannot when praying for them or from a point of spiritual warfare against witchcraft, so it is vital to realise that as you submit to the Lord, His authority remains yours and you may utilise that at will against the powers of darkness. So, all demons are under our feet as well and must submit to our God given authority (Ephesians 1:19-23, Luke 10:19, Romans 16:20).

Authority Through Obedience

Suppose I gave a task to my employee to get new stock for the company, should he come back and say 'could you please do it for me' instead? That doesn't make sense because I have entrusted the task to him. Similarly, the church at large has not stepped into their rightful inheritance by using the dominion and authority that has been given to them. This pertains to all healing, preaching of the Kingdom, deliverance, dead raising and cleansing of lepers. Jesus told us in John 5:19 that He can do nothing by Himself but instead He can only do what He sees His Father doing. If Jesus, the Son of God was required to see what the Father was doing before acting how much more so do the Seer Prophets? Many times we have seen, but did not recognise that it was the Father showing us what He was doing. And that is fine since we are all learning and growing into the fullness of Christ. But to make sure we do not miss it, we should make it a primary task to enter into the secret place daily for the guidance of the Holy Spirit. Obedience to the voice of God is paramount to our success as a child of God and there is a greater expectation upon prophets since they are able to hear secrets from the voice of God more readily than others and not only by an inner witness but by hearing, seeing and feeling in the spirit.

The Kingdom mandate requires us to go to all nations baptising people in the name of the Father, the Son and the Holy Spirit, and teaching them to obey everything Jesus has commanded us (Matthew 28:19-20). This is the commission that the Lord has given us, which applies to every child of God and not merely evangelists. As in the previous example of the employee, it would be wrong for us to ask God to do something He told us to do, knowing we are the body of God on the Earth. It is correct though, to ask to be used by God in greater measures since as sons of God, we will be used without measure to the extent that we desire and allow Him to use us. In Mark 16:17 Jesus says in His name we will cast out demons, speak with new tongues, take up serpents, drink any deadly thing and not be harmed by it, and lay hands on the sick to see them recover. Consider that it does not say pray for the sick, nor pray for demons to be cast out. But God unlocks the ability to do it by giving us permission and authority to do it. These should be natural abilities. A prince can tell his servant to do something and expect it to be done.

Let's take a well-known verse and see why we need eyes to see the prophetic and revelatory information embedded within the word and in essence hear the voice of the Lord.

Jesus says in Mark 11:23 (NKJV), *'For assuredly, I say to you, whoever says to this mountain, 'Be removed and be cast into the sea,' and does not doubt in his heart, but believes that those things he says will be done, he will have whatever he says.'*

This requires no praying; this verse simply states what to do to exercise our authority. Prayer then, should primarily be used for communion with God to understand more of the scripture and to know Him more and secondarily to ask God things that are not in your ability to do, such as asking the Lord to appear in a dream to someone else. That might sound far-fetched, but I have had that prayer answered for myself and others several times. He has already given you the ability to speak over matters in the Earth, the body, soul, spirit and all that has life in it, to cause it to change. Although this verse Mark 11:23 is filled with tonnes of revelation and there are different ways of interpretation given by wisdom of the Holy Spirit, I want to point out a specific revelation as we dive into the wisdom of this verse. I will expound on the idea of not having to ask God for things that we have already been given instruction, authority, power and ability to do ourselves. To understand these things, we must ask for wisdom at times and that is where prayer and communion with God come in. Remember that we build upon each other's revelations and there is no right and wrong, only what is intended for love and life to the edification of the church. This verse Mark 11:23 should be taken literally according to a Greek mindset but also figuratively according to the *Hebraic* mindset. This is of utmost importance to a prophet's understanding and especially one that sees more often in images in the soul, since the voice of God in dreams are displayed more figuratively and more literally in visions. The mountain is usually an obstacle, a hindrance to healing, the casting out of demons or life's obstacles is cast out by what we speak out through our tongue where the power of life and death is (Proverbs 18:21). It is thrown into the sea which represents things that we can overcome such as sins (Micah 7:19), unclean/demonic spirits (Mark 5:13) and strongholds (Isaiah 23:11) etc. We see metaphors amongst other typology of this as Jesus walks on the sea and calms the winds that caused the waves to buffet the boat (Matt 14:22-33). The sea can represent many different facets of the Kingdom but in this context, it speaks of what we can overcome. This demonstrates the overcoming nature of walking on the issues that bound us through the sin nature and worries of life. Mark 11:23 then proceeds to state that there should be no doubt in the heart. For a man of God to have complete dominion they cannot have lingering doubt in the belief/reasoning centre which is the heart. Most people believe that we think in our brain, but we actually think in our heart and the blood flow from the heart carries the thoughts and intents of the heart to our brain which acts as a CPU or processing centre to relay what is in our heart out through our mouth. For out of the abundance of the heart the mouth speaks (Matt 12:34, Luke 6:45, Mark 2:8, Luke 5:22). Finally, Mark 11:23 ends by stating that 'he will have whatever he says'. I will expound on the power of our words in later chapters, but I want you to see here that there was no praying for the situation to change, in actuality, healing, demonic deliverances, the change of life's circumstances and other things is changed by what we say.

Consider this then, should we pray for healing? Should we pray for a demon to be cast out? Should we pray for the dead to be raised? No, we should realise our authority and speak at it as one with the authority to tell those situations or obstacles what to do. The majority of the time church goers begin by saying 'Lord I pray that so and so is blessed or healed', rather than exercising our God-given authority. There is nothing wrong with that. The good thing is that the Lord is lenient with us since we are growing in our understanding and sonship and doesn't hit us over the head with the bible, although figuratively speaking that is what we need. We need the word of God to transform our minds (Romans 12:2).

Using Faith

Everyone starts out with a certain measure of faith; however, it can be grown and needs to be grown for us to manifest as sons of God. How do we get to a point of growing in faith and using the authority and power that is required of us to do the works of God? The disciples asked in John 6:28-29 NIV *'What must we do to perform the works of God'*. Jesus replied, 'The work of God is this: to believe in the One He has sent.' We need to believe that the Lord is true to keeping His word and that He will back up His word with proof.

Mark 16:20 NIV says, *'Then the disciples went out and preached everywhere, and the Lord worked with them and confirmed his word by the signs that accompanied it.'*

It is through the power of the name of Jesus that God will perform healings, miraculous signs and wonders by working with us (Acts 2:22, Acts 4:30, Romans 15:18-19, Mark 16:17). This being your positional authority within the name and on behalf of the name of God.

Hebrews 11:1 NKJV *'Now faith is the substance of things hoped for, the evidence of things not seen'.*

Seer Prophets gain revelation from God primarily through what they see so they can believe completely because of the source from whom they have seen, that being God. It is no longer in the faith realm but now in the love relationship and obedience realms where action is required based on what is seen through dreams, visions and seeing in the spirit. There is a full authoritative knowing that destroys all other belief systems once a revelatory vision is given. Faith therefore is not a matter of mustering up enough belief, that is impossible to do but simple demonstration of action is required. Healing the sick, casting out demons and exercising faith should become synonymous to breathing and walking. These are in fact minor works compared to what we will do when we begin operating in the Heavenly realms in times beyond Jesus' return. The function of a bird's wings is the ability to fly, likewise with the Seer Prophet, once they see with their spiritual eyes and engage the revelatory realm, they can do whatever they see. Healing the sick is a simple act of obedience, lay hands or speak the word. We should not add to the equation by adding doubt or wondering 'what if'. The *Greek* mindset has caused us to falter in this area and so we should return to the *Hebraic* mindset to see and do as Jesus saw and did what His Father did.

So how do we release the power of faith? Let's explore this by using an equation. Desire plus imagination plus the spoken word of God equals creative substance. When God created the Earth, He didn't just speak. Before speaking He obviously had the desire to create Earth, imagined what Earth was to look like, (a representation of Heaven) and then spoke. So, when we exercise faith why do we leave out the essential imagination part of it? Seer Prophets usually see through the imagination which is the beginning point of seeing in the spirit, they then desire/intend it and then speak to create from what is not seen in the physical plane which is substance seen in the Kingdom realm.

Governmental Childlikeness

We should not get confused, the Kingdom of God is righteousness, peace and joy in the Holy Spirit (Romans 14:17). The Kingdom of Heaven is the governmental arena of Heaven. It is not Heaven itself. Heaven is a place of existence such as Earth. We cannot enter the Kingdom of Heaven unless we become like a little child (Matthew 19:14). Why is this? What the Lord is talking about here is entering into everything under the governing rulership of God's government. It requires us to have the simple trust and belief of a child and not a prideful, political mindset.

Jesus says in Matthew 16: 19 (NIV), *'I will give you the keys of the Kingdom of Heaven; and whatever you bind on Earth shall have been bound in Heaven, and whatever you loose on Earth shall have been loosed in Heaven.'*

These are legal matters pertaining to the records of Heaven that are to be administered on the Earth. The carnal mind is at complete enmity against such spiritual perceptions (Romans 8:7) and so we should set our mind on things above and not below (Colossians 3:2). This requires us to take captive any mindsets that come against the knowledge of all things pertaining to God, His ways and works (2 Corinthians 10:5).

Courts of Heaven

Heaven is where all things on Earth was first formed. Sin however is not from Heaven, it is a perversion and a twisting of the truth of what God intended it to be. Our Earthly governments have begun to become twisted mixing demonic mentalities as law and separating itself from the laws of God. As prophets, we carry the testimony of Jesus and testify to His governing acts and rulership. We have the ability to stand before God as Judge in the courts of Heaven which take higher precedence than any governmental court on the Earth and to gain approval, contracts and scrolls to administer upon the Earth. Everything is rigged in your favour as an heir and a son of God. Developing the eyes of your spirit allows you to see the court's proceedings and take part in court sessions. There are many books that have been made regarding the courts of Heaven and all Kingdom governing matters as a Seer should be dealt with first in the Courts of Heaven before taking action in the physical. God calls each person into their assignments and so if you have been given governmental authority over regions you may decree and declare on behalf of regions and pull down powers and principalities accordingly. However, it is best not to play around with such matters unless that Lord has called you to be a representative on the Earth for such matters since you can receive backlash from demonic principalities. Jesus has been given all authority in Heaven and Earth and called us into oneness with Him, therefore we should grow up into all that He is but start off at the level of faith that He has begun us at. We have all received a measure of faith. Through relationship and invitation by the Lord you will be able to grow in authority. Even the most minor demons require that you have an intimate relationship with God to be able to exercise your authority as mentioned before with the seven sons of Sceva. So, let Matthew 6:33 be stamped across your forehead.

Activation

Take time to practice entering into the courts of Heaven. Begin by standing, worshipping and speaking in tongues. Imagine stepping forward from this realm into the courts of Heaven. Cover yourself with the blood of Jesus and stand in the authority of the name of Jesus Christ. Picture the Father as judge, the court's witnesses, Jesus as your advocate and Holy Spirit with you. Ask whatever you would that you know needs to be asked and see Father God slam down the hammer saying, 'it is done'. Practice doing this often and asking the Holy Spirit for greater insight and ability to see clearly and perceive the court's processions.

Take time to exercise faith. Remember desire plus imagination plus the spoken word of God equals creative substance. Have faith in God and trust that whatever you ask according to the will of God shall be done for you. If you don't start using the authority that you have been given you will look back from eternity and say, 'I could have done so much more, if only I tried'.

Prayer

Lord deliver me of false belief patterns and help me to understand the authority that I have been given. Lead me in my prophetic abilities and help me to see into Kingdom Realms and the spirit and begin to call forth from the spiritual plane to the Earthly plane. Help me to perceive and believe like a child and to exercise governmental authority as I grow into full maturity as a son of God made in Your image. Help me to be diligent in setting time aside to be with You Jesus so that I may be filled and commissioned with power and authority to cast out demons with ease and to walk over all the plans of the enemy. In Jesus name. Amen!

5

The Power Of Words As Frequency

Seer Prophets that have been hidden away for training are arising to the public eye in this time, where they have been mandated by God to pave the way forward for all sons of God to see into Kingdom realities and to be taught how to access Heaven at will to be able to live from Heaven to Earth. Right now, the world's fascination with superheroes is a symbolic representation of the revelatory reality that we are to walk in. In the progression of fuel and technology, we have seen man move from coal to electricity, from manual labour, to machinery and to automated robotics. Now we will step into the utilisation of light and frequency. The greatest level of revelation we have of all things in its truest form is frequency. When we understand this, we can then grasp the idea of its functionality and increase our ability to use it to redeem at the genetic level to form things at the greatest level, that being light. Even the lowest forms of bacteria are subject to our domain. As we have been given the power of life and death in our tongue, the very action of creating sound is in itself frequency. This is why saying curses out of anger has power to hurt or degrade others and equally so with the ability to speak life from a place of joy. Even without the elements of emotion and intent, those realities of speaking life and death still operate.

The first thing God says in the bible is, 'Let there be light'. Going by the law of first mention, what the first real thing in the making of Heaven and Earth, was the sound of God's voice, which is frequency and then light appeared. Now this pertains to the account of the Heavens and the Earth. People think that God's original abode is in Heaven, but that is not true, God is greater still and His original abode is from a greater reality known as Eternity. I cannot speak more than I currently have experiential knowledge of, so I will not speak of what Eternity is like, but I can speak of Heaven, it's government and who we were intended to be in the first place. We were birthed in God from Eternity, but we will need to grow up into all things as mature Sons of God to be able to access such beautiful truths. But know this, we are the very house of God, His temple and we are to be able to cross dimensions and planes of existence, being able to have multiple forms of bodies on Earth, in the Heavens and beyond. When Father God, Jesus The Son and Holy Spirit decided to make us in their own image, He called us to be exactly like God in every way. A three part being. This also means that we are 'creative light' that can create as He does. How is that possible? Why are we so important? Even David in the Psalms exclaimed 'What is man that You are mindful of Him?' But since Jesus came, we are no longer mere mortals under the compulsion of sin and death as Paul says. He further says that we will judge angels and His courts and are required to eat meat which is symbolic of growing up into who we were created to be as rulers of the Heavens and not merely drinking milk and worrying about worldly things (1 Corinthians 3:1-4). Gaining a reign on our tongue, our thoughts and intents and ruling our soul and body through the power of the Spirit is essential for us to resonate at God's frequency and that is where we are being called back to. The blood and body of Jesus is the redemptive power and portal to engage the DNA of God and begin to manifest as Sons of God. Once we begin to align ourselves correctly through the Spirit we will begin operating in greater supernatural dimensions. We have indeed stepped into the time Daniel saw in the vision which revelation was closed up until the last days before Christ's return. What a beautiful thing it will be to fly and be caught up with Jesus (1 Thessalonians 4:17, Isaiah 60:8). The things portrayed in movies will be child-play compared to what we will be able to do in times to come. We are indeed eternal beings with a destiny far greater than just living in the now on the Earth. We will speak and create substance as God does, ruling and reigning with Christ. I have made reference to speaking to the mountains in our life as metaphorical notions, but do we truly have such power to literally speak to a mountain and cause it to obey? Yes! In fact, you are so powerful, that your physical Body, Soul and Spirit required the God of all creation to lay aside His divinity, become a man and take upon Himself our sin nature to restore you back to eternal life and divinity. If God had let man continue to eat from the Tree of Life after eating from the Tree of the Knowledge of Good and Evil, in the fallen, sinful state we would live forever as evil divine beings controlling the Heavens and even orchestrating the Courts of Heaven with evil and selfish intent. We see that enough with the manipulation of government on the Earth through the love of money. So that is why satan was cast out to Earth, inside of time because God needed to constrain the sin nature into a period of time since outside of Earth there is no time, it is eternal. It is no wonder that we were kicked out of the Garden at the beginning. We would have been accessing both the Heavens and Earth in a sinful state, carrying corruption throughout all of existence instead of bearing the true identity of God and misrepresenting Him to all of creation both in the Earth and the Heavens. Your body is so important because of this and must be resurrected so that you are able to operate in the physical plane, the spiritual and all Kingdom realms. Your body is a gateway to other dimensions and is able to navigate through different realms. The devil and occult world hide this in plain sight in movies. In actuality, it is perverted to a lesser truth. The greater truths are only revealed by consistent relationship with Holy Spirit and allowing Him to lead you into all truth (John 16:13). This is where our words come in. It contains frequency and the breath of God!

Our words frame our reality. What you let out of your mouth has the ability to terraform the environment, to change mindsets and belief systems, to permeate through darkness and reveal light. Satan stole certain mysteries when He was cast out of Heaven. This pertains to certain mysteries that he was in charge of, so it did not get released to the average believer. For example, as one who was in charge of music hid the powers of frequency governed by music. The truth behind musical notes and frequency is that every note opens a door in the Heavenly realms. Let's take an example, a scale of an octave has seven keys and the eighth is the beginning of the next scale. Seven in Hebrew represents perfection and eight represents new beginnings. But if you add the sharps and flats there are 12 notes, which is the number for divine government. This of course pertains to the reality of music that we can hear with our ears on Earth. Inside of each scale's frequency, therefore is the reality to release perfection into the governmental arenas of the Earth to release the Kingdom. In gaining revelation of these frequencies, we have the redemptive process being released. For example, when Jesus raised Lazarus from the dead, He groaned within Himself (His Spirit) before speaking to raise him from the dead (John 11:33-45). As you can see there is nothing religious about doing such a thing, in fact the Pharisees who were the religious people were intimidated by Him performing these miracles the way He did and still giving thanks to God the Father. It may have looked like abnormal behaviour because there was no long prayer like we have done in churches, or worship music or a holy atmosphere and there was no 'please God' mentality. What it would have looked like was a man making some funny sound, crying because he cared for Lazarus and then tell them to roll the stone away so He could see his cousin's dead body one last time. But here's a Kingdom perspective, in John 11:42 He only audibly thanked God so the people around knew glory was given to the Father and He spoke with authority and a command to dead Lazarus, in fact He only cried because as any loving, compassionate friend or family member we may cry simply because we see one another crying and hurting from a bad situation. This is most likely because they lacked the belief that He was 'the resurrection and the life' standing right in front of them. So, to analyse the truth, through the groaning process (a frequency made from within your belly - where rivers of living water reside), the Spirit is stirred and prays on behalf of us and releases what we cannot find words to perform (Romans 8:26). Such a reality we have by governing frequencies, through the power of our tongue. In this context sound precedes the activity, as with the first words spoken by God to create light. Paul said to Timothy to stir up the gift within you, speaking of the stirring of power through frequency of speaking in tongues and inherently groaning to administer the leading and redemptive power of the Holy Spirit (2 Timothy 1:6-7). Everything was created by the words of God. The devil can only pervert, so we see music used in both the occult, mainstream and church arena. However, the true purpose and nature of it is the underlying frequency which in essence is life and God who is light. Have you noticed that people who listen to certain music dress and act according to the culture presented therein?

In mass crusades or even church gatherings, we have seen pastors operating under an anointing that releases immense power. If the devil can release power without prayer to God shouldn't we who have God living inside of us be able to release much greater power. We often see power released with music and worship of God in the background, followed by a wave of the Pastor's hand or a proclamation of 'FIRE' to release the built-up power. The church has been extremely good at stirring up massive amounts of power, opening the portals of Heaven in their midst and even the presence of God which is actually a release of His frequency. But they have stopped short of the use of it due to the lack of understanding. The occult world has been a step ahead in this area for too long and that needs to change. The church has been going through an awakening. In fact, the whole world has. Have you noticed that there are sometimes several different denominational churches or religious buildings in the same area? This is because the occult world knows how to siphon power from the church. I used to attend a church that had a freemasonry building directly opposite it across from the highway. There was also another Jehovah witness building a few houses down on the same street of that masonry building. Is that a coincidence? No, they purposely positioned themselves to siphon power from unused energy and frequencies created by the praises of people in churches. Have you noticed that churches always need aircon because of the tremendous heat generated? You may often feel heat generated when healing takes place, or the power of God is released onto your body. In fact, your body is like a battery generator, generating higher heat signatures and higher frequencies when in deep praises to God. This is what shows that it is by no means a religious thing, but instead a greater depth of spirituality. I will explain deep realms of prayer in later chapters that give us the ability to resonate at God's frequency.

So, what can we do about functioning correctly? We need to gain a firm understanding of frequencies, the ability of the Spirit's groans, and how to release it. Speaking to God about His ways, is a key component of this and speaking in tongues often will enable you to operate with these untapped frequencies. The powers of the age to come will be governed by these Kingdom realities. We will begin to function at what we were intended if we maintain a diligent relationship with the Source of creation.

The presence of God and the glory of God are in itself forms of frequency where a multitude of different manifestations can occur. Living and abiding in God's presence is where we find the true source of life as God's frequency permeates throughout our body. Therefore it is very important to speak the truth of God's Word and not lies. When truth is spoken it releases the right frequencies that are compatible with our body, which resonate with the presence of God in our lives. That's why as a Christian we are able to perceive when lies are spoken and when we hear truth it settles right in our spirit, and often we even get excited at powerful truthful words spoken in services.

Have you noticed the pain you suddenly feel in your chest after hearing sad or disappointing news? How about the opposite? Have you noticed your whole body enlivens when good news comes? Or when lies are exposed, things in your mind become clearer and you feel a sense of relief? All of these emotions cause a chemical reaction, which is due to the input of a different frequency that is released. Of course, we always want to seek truth and praise God, Jesus is 'The Truth' but unfortunately there are many lies in this world that can cause emotional unrest. Speaking the word of God and truth about your identity will always take you from a depressive state to a jubilant state. Often negative feelings hinder us from proceeding with even beginning to speak good things. Fortunately, God has given a way to combat that by listening to praise and worship songs which carry His presence or His frequency to permeate throughout our being to change our state. I believe when God said 'let there be light' first, it was not by happenstance. Each thing God has done in correct order. So, in actual fact God created frequencies first to govern each area of creation.

There was an experiment conducted that showed the effects of the vibrational patterns of our choice of words. Two glasses were filled with water and spoken to. One was cursed with foul language, the other was blessed with good things. The water was then frozen. Upon looking at both results it was found that the one that was spoken to negatively had severe cracks and an incoherent frozen structure. On the other hand, the positively spoken to water was now smooth with minimal cracks throughout the frozen structure. This is an experiment you can conduct yourself. So, what does this tell us? If our body is made up of at least 60% of water, how we speak to ourselves should matter dramatically. So, the frequencies governed by our voice contain opposing factors depending on truth being spoken or positive words and of course the opposite. The bible says that we have the power of life and death in our tongue

(Proverbs 18:21). This is a very literal concept. You are now the ark of God and your body is the temple of the Holy Spirit. You are a living vessel that not only carries God but has become one with Christ. Prayer is the key therefore to unlock the realms and realities of God to be able to move in untapped dimensions. Remember nothing just happens. You must speak, pray diligently and release the power of God through words and the inherent frequencies.

Ministering With Love

As Seer Prophets we need to learn to put into words what we see. Often, we may struggle to put the things we see into words because it's an image or series of images dropped into our Spirit from God. We may not always have a full understanding of it, but the revelation that is conveyed may come out in stages. If a dream is given to a prophet for another person's life for example, the words spoken need to be governed by love. It is important to take the time to find the words to say in order to deliver the message in a way that the person receiving the word will feel loved and acknowledged by God.

There may at times be reprimanding dreams given and that is not the time for us to ever be a prideful disciplinarian. Instead we should allow the Holy Spirit to convict the person's heart to change that area of their life. Praying and interceding will release the power of God over the person's life. We should declare and prophecy the hope and plans of God for that person, which will create a platform for the manifestation of that prophecy to land in the future. As I said before, nothing just happens, it must be spoken into existence. Just as God speaks and His word does not return void, our words shouldn't either as we bear the same breath and life-giving abilities.

So shall My word be that goes forth from My mouth; It shall not return to

Me void, But it shall accomplish what I please, And it shall prosper in the thing for which I sent it. (Isaiah 55:11 NKJV)

Activation

Take the time to plan how you ought to speak from now onwards. If you begin to tame your tongue, your words will carry more substance, authority and power. When you speak it will have meaning and it will create, especially if we learn to steward it the way God requires it to be stewarded. Take time to pray in tongues often and then pray, do not merely pray from the carnal nature, but instead pray with the things of the spirit in mind so that what you perceive in the spirit may manifest.

Prayer

Lord help me to be attentive to my choice of words and especially how I answer people. Let no foul thing be upon my lips but let my words bring You glory as I speak and manifest creative light and love with my words. May I recognise the same ability in others made in Your image so that I may be attentive to guard my heart if necessary and to encourage godly speech instead. Teach me Holy Spirit to keep a reign on my tongue and speak life-giving words from now onwards. In Jesus name I ask, Amen!

6

Interpreting The Prophetic

Every prophet functions in a greater capacity by the unique way that God chose to give them. That doesn't mean they can't hear from God in a different means. For example, some speak in English some in French but the ones who speak in English as their mother tongue can still learn French and vice versa. This is the same with dreams, visions, words of knowledge, bubbling over with prophetic utterance or anything else. It also matters what types of messages you are required to deliver to people and where you have been positioned as your platform for your calling. For me I have received insight into key events in the world via dreams, visions, hearing the voice of God, and manifested signs and wonders. And I have received ridiculous signs that I can't even begin to fathom how God did it. But that's what makes it more authentic and real because some things need to be a 'wonder' so that God will get the glory. I often get dreams and visions about people as well either to confirm the path they are taking or give a loving rebuke. Unfortunately, no one likes discipline at the time even if it's from God but later on it produces a harvest of righteousness (Hebrews 12:11). Most often God makes me aware of how to interact with certain people either by visions or an inner witness. These are extremely hard to convey to people especially if they are ruled by the carnal mind and have no grid for the prophetic. So, in growing in the prophetic, understanding and interpreting how the Lord speaks to us each individually is vital. He is a Father and He values uniqueness, hence why He talks so uniquely to each of us.

So, let's dive into the need for stewarding the voice of God. We need to recognise that we are not created for ourselves. We were created for each other. The Lord first calls us to be with Him to learn how to commune with Him for ourselves and then for others. Holy Spirit lives in us for ourselves but is on our life for others. Since this is the case, we ought to learn how God speaks to us since God speaks to prophets in riddles. We all aspire to see the Lord and speak face to face, but we have to start where we are at, and not bite off more than we can chew. We need to grow in meekness and humility as Moses did and be very grateful that the Lord even desires to speak with us so much!

'He said, "Listen to my words: "When there is a prophet among you, I, the Lord, reveal myself to them in visions, I speak to them in dreams. But this is not true of my servant Moses; he is faithful in all my house. With him I speak face to face, clearly and not in riddles; he sees the form of the Lord…' (Numbers 12:6-8 NIV)

The Lord loves His prophets, Jesus Himself understood the suffering of disrespect they undergo in their own hometown and the continual backlashes they continue to get (John 4:44). So, we should be considerate that the Lord went through the same treatment from people, especially religious leaders. We should count it a genuine blessing though, since we were handpicked by the Lord and are indeed His friends. Amos 3:7 says that God will not do anything without first revealing it to His servants the prophets. What an honour to be able to perceive the heart and mind of God more readily than others and to pave the way forward as ones carrying the testimony of Jesus. For the testimony of Jesus is the spirit of prophecy!

'And I fell at his feet to worship him. But he said to me, "See that you do not

do that! I am your fellow servant, and of your brethren who have the testimony of Jesus. Worship God! For the testimony of Jesus is the spirit of prophecy." ' (Revelation 19:10 NKJV)

When people hear the Lord speaking so directly to them, their heart is always convicted. Because their false beliefs have to be broken down. Since the Lord speaks so often to Seer Prophets in dreams and visions it is imperative to be able to interpret those pictures into proper articulation of speech so that others may understand as well, especially if it is for someone else. This calls for incredible wisdom, insight and understanding on our behalf. Fasting is a major key for a prophet to develop their ability to interpret dreams. Live a fasted lifestyle but also remember to love each other in the process. Fasting is for you and no one else should have to suffer for your own sake or because of your walk with God. Otherwise love is not correctly shown, and love is the goal of our instruction. (1 Timothy 1:5)

Wisdom - The Principal thing

Why are dreams so important? Because dreams can be real! You may not realise it, but your spirit has fought with demons, given praises to God, travelled to Heaven and back, travelled across the Earth and interacted with God. Ever had a Deja Vu experience? Well your body is just catching up to where your spirit has already been! Let's take a deeper look at what can come from dreams.

The Lord appeared to Solomon in a *dream* and told him to ask anything from Him and He will give it. Thank God Solomon answered with the answer that He gave.

And Solomon said: "You have shown great mercy to Your servant David my father, because he walked before You in truth, in righteousness, and in uprightness of heart with You; You have continued this great kindness for him, and You have given him a son to sit on his throne, as it is this day. Now, O LORD my

God, You have made Your servant king instead of my father David, but I am a little child; I do not know how to go out or come in. And Your servant is in the midst of Your people whom You have chosen, a great people, too numerous to be numbered or counted. Therefore, give to Your servant an **understanding heart to judge Your people, that I may discern between good and evil***. For who is able to judge this great people of Yours?" "The speech pleased the Lord, that Solomon had asked this thing. Then God said to him: "Because you have asked this thing, and have not asked long life for yourself, nor have asked riches for yourself, nor have asked the life of your enemies, but have asked for yourself* **understanding to discern justice***, behold, I have done according to your words;* **see, I have given you a wise and understanding heart***, so that there has not been anyone like you before you, nor shall any like you arise after you. And I have also given you what you have not asked:* **both riches and honour***, so that there shall not be anyone like you among the kings all your days. So, if you walk in My ways, to keep My statutes and My commandments, as your father David walked, then I will lengthen your days." Then Solomon awoke, and* **behold, it was a dream.** *(1Kings 3:5-16)*

If the Lord appeared to Solomon in a dream and gave him an impartation of a wise and understanding heart, I think we ought to pay more attention to what our dreams can do for us. Dreams are usually symbolic unlike visions which are more literal. However, in this instance it was a very literal dream! Each thing came to pass, and King Solomon was indeed wise, rich and honourable. I encourage you to pray and ask the Lord to give you dreams like this, He wants to give you whatever you ask. The best thing we can ask for is wisdom and an understanding heart so that we may understand what the voice of the Lord is trying to convey to His people. Prophets have an important job of delivering messages to the body of Christ and for God's people which calls for an understanding and wise heart. Notice again, that thoughts and reasoning happen in the heart.

Literal Dreams

Teaching dreams or revelatory dreams can be quite literal but also have a mix of symbolism especially when Jesus, the Father or Holy Spirit appears to you. At the start of writing this book I had received the title of this book in a dream by simply asking God for it. I trust God that much to answer me always, in whatever way He likes. Try it with any question that you may have. Write the question down somewhere and wait for Him to respond. God will shock you with His goodness!

I then had a life changing dream. There was no symbolism or prophetic pictures in this dream. I was taken into Heaven through a vast amount of water in the sky. Heaven was buzzing with a vibrant, fun atmosphere! There were lively coloured Holograms of people coming out of the walls and people were interacting with it! I was then in a flight training room where we could learn to fly. There were trampolines everywhere and the instructor said it's impossible for you to get hurt here. My parents had come with me into this room. I was then lying down on a trampoline and my mother next to me said to me, 'You know everyone's calling but you don't know yours'. Before I could answer the floor opened up and I fell through into complete darkness. As I continued to fall, across the screen of my mind, almost like a banner, I heard these words in the Spirit 'I HAVE GIVEN YOU GOVERNMENTAL AUTHORITY!'. As I fell in this completely dark place that seemed to go on for eternity, I saw Father God face to face sitting on a throne. Completely radiant, white light, but I could make out every feature of His face and the gold crown on His head. God had answered for me and told me my calling! He looked like a sea captain with a scruffy short but full beard. I was still falling when a guy flew and caught me and took me into a bathroom. He pushed me up against the door. I knew telepathically, spirit to spirit, that what He was about to do, my dad needed to do to me in the natural. He put his hand on my belly and twisted his palm and said, 'unlock authority' and then he put his other hand over my head and said, 'I give you permission'. I woke up and I cried! How could I not! I had the most intense dream, I had seen the face of the Father, but I cried more so because I thought there's no way my dad would believe this! How could I convince him to do what this guy instructed me to do on behalf of God? While I was still crying, I had a clear reply in my spirit saying, 'you don't have to convince him just tell him'. So, I did. And praise God! My dad did not think I was crazy and actually did the same actions that I was shown. Because it seemed like such an important legal moment, I told my dad we would step by faith into the courts of Heaven and do it before God as the Judge. So, we did, and I felt completely different afterwards! I felt dizzy for a moment and then sat down and collected myself. Wow! What an experience. What came out of that I believe I'll see in months and years to come as well with this book.

So, let's talk about this dream for a moment. There were several things I instinctively knew. This was the same cloud of darkness that God wraps Himself in as He spoke to Moses.

Then they said to Moses, "You speak with us, and we will hear; but let not God speak with us, lest we die." And Moses said to the people, "Do not fear; for God has come to test you, and that His fear may be before you, so that you may not sin." So the people stood afar off, but Moses drew near the thick darkness where God was. (Exodus 20:19-21 NKJV)

God wraps Himself in thick darkness so that we can approach and interact with Him in the same form as us-a man. If the full radiance of God was shown, no one could ever approach God and talk to Him face to face. We know from Numbers 12:8 that God spoke face to face with Moses and from Judges 6:22-23 that we will surely not die if we see God face to face. Indeed, our sinful, carnal nature does die, how could we ever live the same after seeing what you were created to look like from the beginning, the very image of the omniscient, omnipotent and omnipresent God! Sons of God are made in His image (Genesis 1:26-28) and have been made gods over Earth to extend the domain of Heaven to Earth. We are able to approach our Heavenly Father's throne freely in time of need and for mercy (Hebrews 4:16). Unfortunately, most of us have grown up being taught by the world and people's mindsets and opinions, rather than hearing first hand from our Creator. Please don't assume that such things are too wonderful for you, ask and the Lord will give you even greater experiences! These experiences I speak of in this book are nothing compared to the people I know who walk in and out of Heaven like Enoch did.

Let's go deeper, I was also completely made aware that God was lonely there. There was no one else around and He so desperately desires family. Having His kids back means everything to Him! It's no wonder He became a man in the body of His Son Jesus, the first-born Son among many to lay down His life to redeem us (Romans 8:28-30). I believe as you are reading these experiences, it will form desire in your heart to know and see God face to face as well! And that desire will give birth to experiencing God in new ways! We are all His sons and it is our rightful inheritance to enjoy all that the Kingdom of Heaven has to offer including an intimate, loving relationship with our Heavenly Father.

Riddle Me This O' Dreamer of the Night...

It is the glory of God to conceal a matter, But the glory of kings is to search out a matter. (Proverbs 25:2)

Why does God do this? God cares about the process and the journey more than the end result. It is in the journey that you seek after God and fall in love with Him. It is where a true relationship is developed. Getting immediate answers does not force you to go in discovery of the heart of God. In the process of doing so, you learn His heart and His ways, and you begin to renew your mind by the mind of Christ. He always stores up secrets for His children! It is not for those that do not belong to the Kingdom of Heaven. The treasure hunt experience is meant to be an enjoyable experience in the pursuit of the wisdom, knowledge and understanding that God has. If we fall into irritation or bewilderment of the riddles of dreams, it is usually because we are trying too hard to get things done in 'our time' rather than in God's time. Patience is the biggest key to growing in love and the process of searching out a matter develops patience, perseverance and character in us. God will reveal the meanings of dreams in time, but it is found in the process of enjoying your relationship with God first rather than letting dreams become your fixation. Our fixation or Fear of God opens all forms of wisdom, knowledge and understanding for us.

So, we should never covet the dreamer's gift or the understanding of dreams more so than the giver. Enjoy the 'Giver' and you will enjoy every gift from Him!

A Life Story Dream

Dreams with symbolism contain meaning for the past, present and future! These riddles are packed full of revelation and can help build your character as well as show you events to come or even contain messages for yourself or people you know from God. Let's look at Joseph in the bible. The dreams given to Joseph are examples for us to learn from. It shows us how symbolic and prophetic objects and actions can be, as well as carrying subjectiveness and objectiveness. But most importantly the first dreams we hear from Joseph is about His future that He carries with Him before His life actually begins at the age of 30. A complete parallel to Jesus' ministry at the age of 30.

Now Joseph had a dream, and he told it to his brothers; and they hated him even more. So, he said to them, "Please hear this dream which I have dreamed: There we were, binding sheaves in the field. Then behold, my sheaf arose and also stood upright; and indeed, your sheaves stood all around and bowed down to my sheaf." And his brothers said to him, "Shall you indeed reign over us? Or shall you indeed have dominion over us?" So, they hated him even more for his dreams and for his words. Then he dreamed still another dream and told it to his brothers, and said, "Look, I have dreamed another dream. And this time, the sun, the moon, and the eleven stars bowed down to me." So, he told it to his father and his brothers; and his father rebuked him and said to him, "What is this dream that you have dreamed? Shall your mother and I and your brothers indeed come to bow down to the Earth before you?" And his brothers envied him, but his father kept the matter in mind. (Genesis 37:5-11 NKJV)

This riddle is explained a little for us. Although we can get much more out of it! We can see the sun, moon and eleven stars were His family. However, it is his mother Rachel and not Leah, since His father Jacob had two wives. His brother's authority resembled by the sheaves were handed over to Joseph and since all His brothers knew how much his Father favoured him, they would have thought that His Father Jacob would put him in charge of his brothers. They would not have fathomed that he would rule over Egypt and that they would come to him in time of the great famine. As Joseph's life went on, he would have continually brought to remembrance this dream to use as hope and an anchor to get through the tough situations He would have to face. In each stage of Joseph's life, thinking upon this dream would have given Him insight as time unfolded. When he was put in charge of everything in Potiphar's house, he may have thought he may get the chance to go back to his family with riches. But when he was thrown in prison for a time, he would have had to hold on again to the dream as an anchor of hope to recalibrate his thoughts. When he finally came out of prison, he was put in charge of all of Egypt and finally the dream came to fulfilment by the time he was 30 years old. Have you had a dream that you always pondered about, waiting and hoping something will come of it? Continue to set the Lord always before you and use the dreams as an anchor of hope that your life is not worthless but has incredible value which will be revealed in due time.

Let's head back to the dream! Why did the family need to resemble stars? We as Christians know the story from reading the word of God, I believe that using stars to resemble the family demonstrated the impact they would all have in the future of Israel. The names of the brothers were given to the tribes of Israel. And we know that God showed Abraham His descendants in the stars. So, we are able to see here that stars are symbolic of believers or children of God. There are many small instances in the bible that interpret themselves. Discover them for yourself as you walk with God and use it for your own dream interpretation dictionary so that you will be able to steward the voice of God well for your life.

Activation

Pray earnestly for God to reveal Himself to you in dreams and be ready for an answer. Be expectant for Him to come to you and ask something along the lines of 'what would you like me to give you'. I pray that the desire of your heart will be for the spirit of wisdom and revelation to grow in the knowledge of the surpassing love and grace of our Lord Jesus Christ. If you have those things you will grow in all areas of your life and be blessed with both riches and honour as well as long life. Then can you be a true blessing to others as you steward the giftings of the Lord.

Take time to write down your spiritual gifts. Ask the Lord to show you important messages for yourself and for others. Remember to right down whatever you perceive from the Lord, as the Lord sees you doing that, He will increase that gifting on your life. Don't squander your talents or bury them in the ground. The Lord is kind so do not be afraid of making mistakes. It is ok to make mistakes, but it is not ok to know that you have a gift and not use it because you were worried that you may offend God in case you got it wrong. God has too much grace, love and mercy and will make sure you grow as you yield to the Holy Spirit.

Take time to steward your dreams, visions, any signs and wonders by asking for confirming words, scripture relations and the ability to understand them with full revelatory knowledge of the voice of God embedded within. Get a journal and begin to write the effects of the exact moments. For example, the date, time, what you were doing, what you were thinking, what you were feeling and what has been happening in your life. That way you will know what the sign and wonder was pointing to and your ability to know what every sign points to will increase.

Prayer

Father I ask in the name of Jesus for the spirit of Wisdom and Revelation to understand dreams, visions, signs and wonders. I ask that I may grow in my spiritual receptivity and obtain a wise and understanding heart to be able to interpret dreams, visions and all things prophetic to be able to govern my life and to assist others as well. I also ask for greater encounters with you, so that I may learn directly from you without any filtering from others. Help me to nurture my relationship with Holy Spirit so that I may discern the voice of God through dreams and come into a place where I will be able to see you face to face. May I grow in meekness and humility as Moses did. So that I will finally be transfigured as Jesus was with His attitude of doing only what He saw You doing. In Jesus name I ask. Thank You Father God. Amen!

7

Strongholds and Hindrances

The greatest of hindrances to our complete functioning as Seers are the demons that set themselves up upon the gateways of our soul. Unfortunately, every person goes through forms of pain that cause them to develop mindsets that are put in place to protect themselves from further pain. It can also come through generational belief systems without your knowledge. These mindsets if undergone continuous trauma, turn into strongholds possessed by demons. Pain, trauma and sin gives legal right to allow demons to infiltrate the soul and this can become so severe that it hinders your ability to be attentive to the voice of God. In John 14:30 Jesus states that 'the devil has nothing in Him'. Likewise, we ought to be the same. Our body belongs to the Holy Spirit. It is His temple (1 Corinthians 6:19). We were bought at a very high price, that being the precious blood of Jesus Christ. Should we then share it with demons? Surely not! And so, the Lord has given us a way to eradicate these demons that set themselves up as strongholds in our soul.

For the weapons of our warfare are not carnal but mighty in God for pulling down strongholds, casting down imaginations and every high thing that exalts itself against the knowledge of God, and bringing into captivity every thought to the obedience of Christ... (2 Corinthians 10:4-5 NKJV).

Repentance, forgiveness, the power of the word of God, the authority of the name of Jesus and the blood of Jesus allows us to bind these demons and cast them out. This will allow us to have the gateways of our soul functioning freely to allow the voice and glory of God to be clearer. God is always speaking, but we can have obstructions to perceiving His voice clearly.

So, this chapter will be a combination of exercises that I have used to help clear my gateways as well as explanations of the threefold nature of man. That being the body, soul and spirit. This is an extremely important chapter of the book to remove as many blockages as possible from our side. If you believe that you are unable to do any of this yourself consider attending deliverance ministry or asking trustworthy Christian elders to assist you. This is not necessarily something you do once and forget about it. It is important to keep short accounts of what you come into contact with once you have cleared the gateways, since living in the world in its current state doesn't make it easy to avoid pain, trauma or sin.

When I had first heard about doing this by using the blood of Jesus to clean the gateways of our soul, I was cautious in case I was doing something wrong. I mean I didn't want to insult God, so I asked for a sign if it was correct. A few nights after asking for the sign, I received a confirmation. As I walked into my bathroom at around midnight, the sink was covered with blood - fresh, alive and bright red! It was splattered throughout the inside of the sink basin. There were thick blood droplets, presented so neatly, it was as if every 1cm there was another drop of blood positioned in alignment. My first thought was maybe someone brushed their teeth and their gums were bleeding, or an insect died, but that didn't make sense, there was too much, too neatly placed throughout the sink and none of it was dry. So, I just decided to wash it out just in case, because I didn't want to embarrass my family. The next morning it was back. Exactly as it was. No one had used my sink. It was obvious this was from God. A few days later I realised that was the sign I had asked for! The voice of God was in the blood in the sink. He was showing me the purification power of the blood to make the gateways clean. I knew I could trust the process and the redemptive power of the blood of Jesus became more real to me than it had ever been! You're probably thinking that this guy must be clueless! Sometimes the shock of a wondrous sign can leave you dumbfounded. You don't always recognise a wonder as a sign at first glance. But all signs and wonders contain the voice of God and we should never be in awe of a sign but rather the love of the one giving the sign as a testimony of Jesus.

To be delivered from strongholds we need to also be delivered first from any demons that have the ability to manifest themselves. So why is there such a need to be delivered from demons? Our body is the temple of the Holy Spirit. It is impure to have other unclean spirits dwelling inside of God's temple. There was a reason that Jesus made a whip and cleared out the temple from trading (John 2:13-16). Your body is meant to be a house of prayer and not a demonic trading floor. Demons are literal spirits with their own personality. When a demon manifests, they don't always speak with a different voice or go into a frantic trance, although that can happen. Most often it comes out in repetitive actions that are demonic in nature, usually with a selfish aspect. *Examples of these can be spirits of pride, anger, lust, control, slander, fear, abusiveness, covetousness, jealousy and many others.* If you are unable to resist doing any of these things you may have one or more demons to get rid of. You need to deal with these as if they are individual persons who have infiltrated your soul. Demons can also latch onto your body and effect it through pain or trauma that you have experienced in the past. Often phantom pain experienced by people who have lost limbs, may have received a spirit of trauma or infirmity causing that pain to occur by bringing back the traumatic pain associated with the memory. These spiritual hitchhikers don't have any good intention and will only increase in strength and number if more pain, trauma or sin occurs. If you become aware that you may have a demon, deal with them as fast as possible since it is vital to your own wellbeing and your walk with Jesus. You cannot experience the fullness of the Kingdom of God without being completely free. I would venture to say that all people, Christian and non-Christians have to be delivered from demons. It is foolishness to think that a Christian cannot have demons. In fact, I believe that Christians need to often check themselves to see if they are walking according to the carnal nature and bind any familiar spirits from invading their families. Once delivered it is important to be filled with Holy Spirit since the Holy Spirit is a seal (Ephesians 1:13). This will prevent demons from returning and returning with seven more wicked than itself. (Luke 11:24-26). To get rid of these demons is a matter of understanding your authority in Christ as I spoke about in previous chapters regarding the seven sons of Sceva. I believe that anyone can deliver themselves because of the authority Christ has given you. Simply believe! Delivering others is a matter of being with Jesus and commissioned by Him as He gave the disciples authority to cast out demons (Matt 10:1). If something pertains to a belief pattern, that in itself is a stronghold which can be taken down by the blood of Jesus and the renewing of the mind (Romans 12:2). You will need to walk others through removing belief patterns. Belief patterns come through a lifestyle and not merely a demon, although it can be governed by a demon. You cannot deliver someone else of the same demon you have. It is hypocritical and satan cannot drive out satan. You must be free yourself to set another free by the authority of Jesus.

Understanding Gateways

Lift up your heads, O you gates! And be lifted up, you everlasting doors! And the King of glory shall come in. Who is this King of glory? The Lord strong and mighty, The Lord mighty in battle. Lift up your heads, O you gates! Lift up, you everlasting doors! And the King of glory shall come in. Who is this King of glory? The Lord of hosts, He is the King of glory. Selah. (Psalm 24:7-10 NKJV)

You are these gates and everlasting doors. We need the Lord to enter and save us from the demons that attack us and ruin our life. Indeed, nothing can stand against the might of the Lord. And we desperately need Him to come as the King of Glory to set up His throne in our gateways. So, I am going to walk you through the gateways and give you examples of what to do. You will need to do this for each of the gateways. The word of God says that out of your belly will flow rivers of living water (John 7:38). This begins from the Kingdom of God within you. It is governed by the First Love Gate. The first love gate is meant to be reserved for Christ.

Revelations 3:20 says *'Behold I stand at the door and knock. If anyone hears my voice and opens the door, I will come in to Him and dine with Him and He with me.*

Once the first love gate is open and cleaned out, the glory of God can come through with ease and permeate to the 8 doors/gateways of the Spirit, then out the 7 gateways of the soul and 5 gateways of the body.

First Love Gate: Glory of God
Spirit gateways: Prayer, Fear of God, Reverence, Intuition, Revelation, Faith, Hope, Worship
Soul gateways: Conscience, Will, Reason, Choice, Imagination, Emotions, Mind (Subconscious; Conscious; Unconscious)
Body gateways: Mouth (Taste), Nose (Smell), Ears (Hearing), Eyes (Sight), Touch (Feel)

As described previously the body resembles the outer court of the temple, the soul the inner court and the spirit the Most Holy place where true communion with God takes place. The body needs to become under subjection to the Kingdom of God behind the First love gate, transforming your spirit and allowing the Holy Spirit's influence. The way to do that is to take charge of your soul through the power of the Spirit. If we continue to rely on gaining information purely from external means i.e. Body to Soul instead of Spirit to Soul, then we will remain in the power of the flesh or carnal nature rather than being Spirit led or walking by the Spirit. As the Word of God says, to be carnally minded is death but to be spiritually minded is life (Romans 8:6-10). Only then can we fully manifest Christ.

Cleansing The Gateways

I am assuming that if you are reading this book you are a born again Christian. If you are not please do not do any of this as Holy Spirit must live inside of you, otherwise you will open your gateways to demons, and you will become open to demonic possession. With that being said repentance and forgiveness must be done through the steps and the authority to use the judgemental power of the blood of Jesus must be yours. Every Christian has that right. If you need to, please make sure you give your life to Christ, the redemptive power of the blood brings righteous judgement and is not to be taken lightly.

Imagination is essential during these steps. Since I have designed this book specifically for growing as prophetic seers it is best to start with the First Love gate as the first example, followed by the spiritual gateway of revelation, the soul gateway of imagination and the body gateway of the eyes. This way you will have a firm foundation to begin taking possession of the other gateways through the same method.

Each level of gateway or doorway requires different things to happen. We will use the two words interchangeably during this chapter. The First Love gate is the most important gateway. It requires us to open it by ourselves to allow the glory of God to come through to all other gates. Often, we set up a guard on this door unknowingly if we have suffered heartbreak due to relationships. My First Love gate looked terrible before I did this! That was because of hurt that came through past relationships and it wasn't functioning as it should. It may at times have chains or blockages we have set up ourselves to prevent us from getting hurt further but that actually hinders its true functioning and relationship capacity with Christ. The spirit gateways may have chains as well. The blood of Jesus can be applied to the spiritual gateways to redeem it and have the chains broken. The soul & body gates may have chains as well as demons. You will need to bind them and cast them off the gateways as shown in the steps in the next section.

First Love Gate & Spiritual Gateways

Let us begin. To open the First Love gate which is reserved for Christ, begin by imagining the door or gate. On the other side of the First Love gate is the Kingdom of God where the glory of God flows freely from. **To think is to do in the realm of the Spirit. So, imagine it being done and it will be done by faith in the spirit.**

1. Pray in tongues for at least 1 minute and continue to pray in tongues during the duration of this. This will stir the receptivity of your spirit.
2. Imagine the door of first love. It will look different for everyone and there is no wrong way of imagining it.
3. Reach out your hand by faith and pull the door open. Or command the door be opened. And visualise it happening.
4. Invite and see the glory and fire of God coming through this doorway having free access to all other doorways. Allow the Holy Spirit to carry the glory of God and consecrate and sanctify them. Ask Holy Spirit to heal you and make each area brand new.
5. Ask Jesus as the King of Glory to set up His throne on the door-

ways, so nothing else may pass and may be subject to His filtering.
6. Continue to do it until you feel a shift in your spirit. You may feel raw or empty inside, which means that it is working, and you may also feel lighter as if you are carrying less burdens since you are.

Repeat for every spiritual gateway thereafter.

Redeeming The Soul & Body Gateways

The difference with the soul and body arena may include demonic strongholds of which can be broken only by the blood of Jesus.

1. Pray in tongues for at least 1 minute and continue to pray in tongues during the duration of this. This will stir the Spirit within you.
2. Imagine each doorway individually.
3. Stand within the positional authority of the name of Jesus break every chain upon the door if there have been chains or blockages setup. Use your words for example 'I break these chains in Jesus name!' Proceed to binding any demons that may sit upon the throne of this gateway. 'I bind every demon of offence, pain and rejection.' Command them to get off and they will because of the authority of Christ in you. Often you will need to forgive those that have wronged you if you haven't already. This will also allow healing to begin.
4. Apply the blood of Jesus by imagining yourself taking a paint brush dipping it into the blood of Jesus and painting over the door completely. Voicing this out works as well.
5. Command the door be opened. And visualise it happening.
6. See the glory and fire of God coming through this doorway having free access to all other door ways. Allow the Holy Spirit to

carry the glory of God and consecrate and sanctify every doorway. Ask Holy Spirit to heal you and make it brand new.
7. Ask Jesus as the King of Glory to set up His throne on the doorway, so nothing else may pass and may be subject to His filtering.
8. Continue to do it until you feel a shift in your spirit. You may feel raw or empty inside, which means that it is working, and you may also feel lighter as if you are carrying less burdens since you are.

Repeat for every soul and body gateway thereafter.

There may be several other methods of doing this. This is just what has worked for me and what has worked for several other people in deliverance ministry. The key things are the power of the blood and the authority of Christ, as well as binding any demons and having them removed from the gateways. As you do this you will begin to experience changes in all areas. It does not always happen overnight, although it can.

For myself when I began working my way through the hearing gate, my mind gate and revelation gate, I began to hear audibly in the spirit to a greater extent. The same with the eyes and imagination gateways. As I began to unlock each of the gateways, I also took upon myself time to fast. That gave me a greater receptivity to the things of the Spirit. We will go onto a deeper explanation of fasting in later chapters. You may notice that you feel less cluttered in your thoughts, thought processes and emotions. This is simply because you are entering into a greater reality of righteousness, peace and joy governed by the initial glory of God inside the Kingdom of God deep within your being. You are also becoming subject to the law of the Spirit of Life in Christ rather than the law of sin and death. You will also be able to remember certain memories and not feel hurt from it. If you notice that certain memories still hold any pain attached to it, you can use the blood of Jesus to paint over those memories to redeem it from any pain. It is important to keep short accounts thereafter of what you come in contact with. I used to hear blasphemous curse words in my head. It was completely demonic and only once I used the power of the blood of Jesus was it gone. In fact, it took me some time to realise that I don't have those other invading voices anymore because I became so free (Isaiah 41:12). My mind was being renewed by the power of the blood of Christ and so can yours.

These are merely tools and a means to clear the gateways so that you can operate from your Spirit outwards. This is a key component to fulfilling the work of God. How do we fulfil the work of God? Simply by believing (John 6:29). If these gateways are not cleared, you will not rely on simply believing. You will end up trying to figure things out and get into a 'works' mentality to try to get God to move when we need to come to the realisation that we are one with Christ and all that He has is ours. Everything has been given to us already pertaining to life and godliness (2 Peter 1:3). We need to bring our flesh and soul under subjection of our spirit (1 Corinthians 9:27), since our spirit is one with Christ (1 Corinthians 6:17).

Do not be afraid if any outward manifestations occur or any strange feelings occur. Continue in the atmosphere of praise and worship to God. Your Spirit's capacity will grow and stretch as you fall under the governing power of the Lord. Yield to the Holy Spirit's power and have your life transformed from the inside out!

If you would like to learn more about cleaning the gateways, Ian Clayton from Son of Thunder has excellent resources to learn from.

Activation

Keep short accounts of what you come into contact with in the world, interacting with others, listening to or watching.

Regularly imagine the gateways and apply the blood of Jesus over it so that it may function well always and your receptivity to the voice of God may be louder and clearer than anything else.

This takes time, but consistency and persistence will bring you results. Ask the Holy Spirit to teach you how to do this correctly, each person has been subject to different things, but the power of the blood of Jesus has power to redeem us from all carnal and demonic things.

Prayer

Father will You please help me to take possession of my gateways correctly and may you give me the discipline to keep short accounts and turn my attention to you rather than being spoiled by the corruption that is in the world. Thank You for making a way to redeem our lives. May we bring You honour and glory. We humbly ask You Jesus as the King of Glory to set up your throne upon the gateways of our body, soul and spirit to govern each entry point. May no other voices linger or persist, but may they be demolished as we pull down every stronghold and every thought that rises against our obedience to Christ. Help us to not hold onto any unforgiveness, but instead may we walk in repentance and purity. In Jesus precious name. Amen!

8

Keys To Growing Prophetic Insight

Holy Spirit Our Greatest Teacher

Everything that we have ever learnt came from someone else and that is one of our biggest mistakes. Reading books, doing courses, hearing explanations from someone else is great but it should never be your source of information. It should only stir you into a greater relationship with Jesus and His beautiful Holy Spirit and confirm what Holy Spirit is teaching you in your spirit. We should be learning primarily all things from Holy Spirit as the word of God says that He will teach us all things. This is not limited to just life and Godliness.

'But the Helper, the Holy Spirit, whom the Father will send in My name, He will teach you all things, and bring to your remembrance all that I said to you (John 14:26 NKJV).

As for you, the anointing which you received from Him abides in you, and you have no need for anyone to teach you; but as His anointing teaches you about all things, and is true and is not a lie, and just as it has taught you, you abide in Him (1 John 2:27 NIV).

Does this mean that we do not need teachers or mentors? By no means, what this means is that Holy Spirit needs to be our primary teacher and everything that we learn pertaining to all areas of life should be weighed up against the truth that Holy Spirit reveals to us. He is our Spirit guide and our filter of truth. God has given us teachers through the five-fold ministry and has told us to test the spirits as well. So, it would be contradictory to say He is the only one allowed to teach us.

So Christ himself gave the apostles, the prophets, the evangelists, the pastors and teachers, to equip his people for works of service, so that the body of Christ may be built up until we all reach unity in the faith and in the knowledge of the Son of God and become mature, attaining to the whole measure of the fullness of Christ (Ephesians 4:11-13 NIV).

Beloved, do not believe every spirit, but test the spirits to see whether they are from God, for many false prophets have gone out into the world. By this you know the Spirit of God: every spirit that confesses that Jesus Christ has come in the flesh is from God, and every spirit that does not confess Jesus is not from God. This is the spirit of the antichrist, which you heard was coming and now is in the world already (1 John 4:1-3 NKJV).

We have also been given the seven Spirits of the Lord as Jesus was given (Isaiah 11:2) to be our governors and tutors until we reach maturity as sons of God (Galatians 4:2) able to govern this house and our Father's household. Only then will we be able to judge angels and His courts (Zechariah 3:7, 1 Corinthians 6:2-3).

The only way to develop a discerning spirit is through maintaining a deep relationship with Holy Spirit. Your spirit and God's are now joined in unity and the words spoken by anyone must resonate with your spirit. When you yield to Holy Spirit and allow your relationship to be developed to such an extent, it becomes very easy to know when people are lying or not. Isn't that cool? Not really! Once you are able to experience such dimensions of reality, you also need to have a relationship with the spirit of wisdom and learn to manage the responsibility that comes with such ability and relationship. Sometimes Holy Spirit will prompt you to hold your tongue even though you know something is not the truth. But do not fear, because truth will always reveal itself in due time. Patience therefore, is the biggest step in growing in prophetic insight and learning the mysteries of God and walking as a son of God. We are called to become the personification of love. It is no wonder that the first thing love is, is patient (1 Corinthians 13:4).

The Functions of Destiny

I was given a dream that I was in another realm above the Earth known as a place called Destiny. I was walking in and out of portals in this plain of existence. I went to restore the people there with my own group of people. They were doing something bad to the whales in the area. But before going further on through the path, I needed to unlock 8 different new powers or functions that were inside of a treasure chest. The treasure chest was inside of these square pillars that were continually changing shape and were wrapped in vines and plants growing on it. After gaining access and unlocking the chest I was then on a high mountain village with the sea in full sight. The people were doing something about the big plants that were growing from the sea affecting the whales.

A bit of a crazy dream don't you think? If you have eyes to see what the Spirit of the Lord is saying here, then it can be a phenomenal dream. It took me 3 months before a friend of mine said something to trigger the revelation of what these 8 powers or functions were. In the previous chapter I mentioned the 8 gateways of the Spirit. I believe these were the 8 functions or powers it was pointing to especially with the treasure chest being in the centre of this place. The chest being my heart and the vines being a hindrance to its full functioning. The sea has many symbolisms but, in this case, I believe it speaks of the worldly things to overcome. And the plants sabotaging the whale speaks of hindrance to the prophetic ministry. Whales are creatures of the ocean or water that represent things of the spirit. They are extremely sensitive to communication, being able to communicate across vast distances and in frequencies that other animals or man cannot fathom. Likewise, with the prophet, being more sensitive to spiritual things than others.

So, the Lord was actually showing me keys to grow as a prophet and the removal of the hindrances of the world by showing me that the real issue is the heart or more importantly the 8 gateways of the spirit. Once I realised this, I was able to grow my prophetic abilities by cleansing the gateways as mentioned in the previous chapter. There are many other things that we can use to grow the prophetic nature however these 8 gateways are the focal points. Just to recap the **Spirit gateways** are: Prayer, Fear of God, Reverence, Intuition, Revelation, Faith, Hope and Worship. All things were given for us to be in relationship with God, having access to all resources and going about our Father's business. Consider, did Jesus lack anything? Was He in perfect relationship with the Father? And was He not testifying to the fact that He was continually about His Father's business, doing only what He saw His Father doing? (John 5:18-20). Let's take a brief look at each gate so that we may function the same way and be in perfect relationship with God and become one with Him. I believe each area deserves its own book, but for the sake of expounding on these 8 gateways/functions I will touch on them briefly.

Prayer

What is prayer and what is it not? Prayer is not us begging God for things to accommodate our life. It is our submission unto the will of God as Jesus said '...not my will but yours be done (Luke 22:42)'. Prayer was given as a means of communication between the Father and His sons, so that we may become one with Him and have the ability to talk face to face with our Heavenly Father as we go about our Father's business. Once we begin to yield ourselves fully to the leading of Holy Spirit and His means of *unique* communication to each of us, we will be able to have an answer for every aspect of our lives. It may seem grandiose, but I assure you if we yield ourselves to continual prayer and maintain a life lived out of the ever proceeding word of God, we will function as gods made in the image of our Father. Jesus is our example of what we were meant to look like on the Earth. Should we live below our highest potential? Surely, we should aim to live at everything we were created to be in the first place. That begins simply by talking to God and taking the time to *listen* for His reply. Prayer should in fact be 1% us talking and 99% of listening to what God is saying in reply. Let's take a quick look at the example prayer that Jesus gave us.

In this manner, therefore, pray: Our Father in Heaven, Hallowed be Your name. Your Kingdom come. Your will be done on Earth as it is in Heaven. Give us this day our daily bread. And forgive us our debts, As we forgive our debtors. And do not lead us into temptation, But deliver us from the evil one. For Yours is the Kingdom and the power and the glory forever. Amen. (Matthew 6:9-13 NKJV)

This is merely a template to guide our prayers. We are in fact calling forth His will to be done on the Earth. A very literal statement for Heaven to invade Earth in every way possible. We really shouldn't over complicate things, God simply wants relationship and He wants to take care of us, but we limit Him. We don't realise how powerful we are that we can stop God from operating in our lives because we choose to be our own god by default. When we try to figure things out on our own or try to protect or provide for ourselves, we are in fact saying, 'I don't need God to be my source for everything!'. We ought to talk to Him in any way we can but growing the relationship is the point of it all and He will guide us into praying powerful prayers that can literally shake the world! When we begin to take responsibility for our assignments, we can trust that God will guide us, our prayers shall be answered because it is in alignment with His will and it is not out of selfishness. There is much to say about prayer, maybe that will be left for another book. Keep it simple, you are His kid, and desire is the simplest starting place. Your prophetic abilities grow simply from being able to *communicate well* with God.

A beautiful quote by A.W. Tozer: *'When the eyes of the soul looking out meet the eyes of God looking in, Heaven has begun right here on this Earth'*

Fear of God

An easy way to understand what the Fear of the Lord is, is to ask yourself 'Do I care more about what God thinks than my own opinion or other's opinion? Or, does it bother me whether I offend God or not? When we are able to show such respect to such an extent to God, we by default have the Fear of God. Can we truly serve and love a God because of the demonic spirit of fear? Definitely not! Those are very separate issues of fear. But there are two results of the true fear of the Lord for His children and for sinners.

The fear of the Lord is to hate evil; Pride and arrogance and the evil way. And the perverted mouth, I hate. (Proverbs 8:13 NKJV)

The real fear of the Lord will give sons of God wisdom because we care more about what He says on a matter rather than our own mind or others. When people speak from truth and the fear of the Lord, it is authoritative and will result in change.

The fear of the Lord is the beginning of wisdom, And the knowledge of the Holy One is understanding. (Proverbs 9:10 NKJV)

I believe that your true-life calling cannot start until you begin to have the Fear of the Lord. The reason I say this is because everything you do without discovering the reason for your existence from your creator, you as the creation cannot begin to function as you were intended to. You must delve into the mind of your creator to know your function otherwise everything else surmounts to trial and error or guessing what your functions are for.

As a prophetic individual living from your spirit is key. We cannot live according to external circumstances. But instead we ought to respond based on what God is doing first and then towards the physical life. The fear of the Lord therefore promotes life and not death since our goal is to be led by the Spirit rather than the carnal nature.

The fear of the Lord is a fountain of life, That one may avoid the snares of death. (Proverbs 14:27 NKJV)

However, the fear of the Lord to a person who rejects God should be a truly frightening experience. Unfortunately, sin makes people blind to the frightening justice of the Lord against sin. So, consider the beauty of the wisdom of God, that though He as judge must deal with sin, He uses that same fear to teach a son of God as a tool of wisdom, knowledge and understanding. It is only when we realise that we as sons of God are without sin, can we divide the two resulting outcomes and realise how blessed we are!

Jesus says: 'And do not fear those who kill the body but cannot kill the soul. But rather fear Him who is able to destroy both soul and body in hell. "Are not two sparrows sold for a cent? And yet not one of them will fall to the ground apart from your Father. But the very hairs of your head are all numbered. Do not fear therefore; you are of more value than many sparrows.' (Matthew 10:28-31 NKJV)

The prophetic call does not operate without the fear of the Lord. In retrospect we operate under the title of witchcraft if any form of prophecy is done contrary to the fear of the Lord. God ordains prophets before the womb. The gifting on your life is therefore up to you, to operate as a false prophet governed by demonic influence or to function with the wisdom of God. By default, if there is no fear of the Lord, there is fear of another god(idol) that you have established without realising in your life.

Reverence

Reverence is honour, awe, respect and concern for the things of God. As a result, reverence produces holiness, purity and righteousness. Grace is a by-product of reverence, it is given to empower us to fulfil our assignments and to overcome life's adversities and sins. Consider then if we seek first the Kingdom of God and Jesus' righteousness, are not all things added unto us? (Matthew 6:33). In contrast, to have disdain for the things of God does not supply holiness, purity or righteousness, so grace to overcome sin or life's adversities is not given. So, if grace were to be given without repentance or change it is demonic and wasn't true grace at all.

The prophetic call is always in conjunction with the priestly duty. As we have been called to be Kings and Priests in the new covenant, we are all liable under the governing of its principles. The Lord made a covenant with Levi to have life and peace. This required them to have the greatest of reverence for God. The priestly tribe descended from Levi. As a community of priests, they were required to live set apart unto reverence of God leading by example of what all men are to come to. The outcome of such reverence was truthfulness, peace and uprightness and the wisdom to turn many from sin.

My covenant was with him, a covenant of life and peace, and I gave them to him; this called for reverence and he revered me and stood in awe of my name. True instruction was in his mouth and nothing false was found on his lips. He walked with me in peace and uprightness and turned many from sin.

For the lips of a priest ought to preserve knowledge, because he is the messenger of the Lord Almighty and people seek instruction from his mouth. (Malachi 2: 5-7 NIV)

Intuition

Intuition allows us to instinctively discern what is truth or what is right without the need for any forms of reasoning. For example, have you ever known exactly what someone else was thinking without them speaking? That is called cardiognosis. The ability to know the thoughts and intents of the heart. As Christians, we have the influence of Holy Spirit governing our intuitiveness which allows us to make right decisions without having to weigh pros and cons or be justified through natural reasoning. This is very important since we as prophetic people need to rely on this ability of intuition in ministry, interpreting dreams or visions and especially discernment of spirits. Did Jesus operate in cardiognosis? Definitely! God is omniscient but Jesus came as a man who was required to be baptised with the Holy Spirit as well. So, we too can know the thoughts and intentions of people's hearts.

But immediately, when Jesus perceived in His spirit that they reasoned thus within themselves, He said to them, "Why do you reason about these things in your hearts? (Mark 2:8 NKJV).

Intuitiveness does not come from growing in the prophetic or is it gained with more knowledge. It comes from relationship with Holy Spirit and the spirit of wisdom and counsel so that what the Lord reveals to you will be to glorify Himself. Likewise, we are also required to keep the majority of things we discover to ourselves since even mature Christians are unable to handle certain secrets. When you care about nothing else apart from becoming love as God is love and being one with Him, walking in the fullness of what He created you for and finally a sincere desire to walk in purity, truth and the spirit, you will begin to function like your Heavenly Father. God living inside of you can tell Himself anything if He can see Himself in you, meaning His character because He trusts Himself in you. Growing in this area of life requires the utmost desire for truth, love and desire to protect others from deceit. Unfortunately, a tremendous amount of caution needs to be exercised since it is very easy to get belittled because you know key truths pertaining to life, godliness and people's hearts, and you are unable to explain how you know these things other than say 'God told me so'. This of course is an excellent reason for such intuitiveness! But religion, scepticism and the carnal minded nature of others will easily come against this ability of intuitiveness with arguments and reasoning. Even mature Christians can find it hard to accept this kind of intuition if they themselves have not grown into this aspect of life.

Often those that are highly intuitive will receive secrets and mysteries from God that only they can handle, not because they are smarter or better than others, but in fact quite the opposite, they care about personifying love, meekness and righteousness. For sons of God to be allowed to handle true intuition they must not have the need to be right or have the need to correct others. Their life and character must convict others by the power of love and selflessness rather than opening their mouth to correct because of the knowledge of right and wrong. Having a relationship with the Lord like this is truly intimate but requires sincere desire for purity. Please understand that purity is not the ability to not sin, it is having no double mindedness but instead sole attention and devotion to the truth of God's Word. It is also known as reckless abandonment as some would call it. If ever we can say that we are pure enough in our motives and therefore deserve the abilities of cardiognosis, future insight, the ability of understanding times and seasons or knowing things that we couldn't possibly know at all then we would be gravely mistaken. To grow in intuitiveness, we must grow in meekness. As Moses was the meekest person in all the world, God was able to show him His ways and appear to Him. This of course was before Jesus.

'Now the man Moses was very meek, above all the men which were upon the face of the Earth' (Numbers 12:3 NKJV).

There are not many people of such meekness that I know who operate out of such revelation and intuition, however those that do intrinsically exercise love and caution, and never appear to act as if they know it all. I believe that to have such ability from God only comes from resigning yourself from opinion and choosing God's opinion and truth to reign in your mind and disregarding all opinions and negative thoughts of others. Even to the point of not having to correct or judge others but simply love and enjoy the created value of others. Then as they see Christ in you, they are convicted by the Holy Spirit automatically. Intuition can't be figured out, we must give ourselves over to the mind of Christ. There is much to say about intuition, but it will mean nothing if we desire it just to act like we know everything or appear to be more highly gifted than others. Motives have to be squeaky clean and that comes from a life of resigning to the ever-proceeding word of God for yourself and others.

He who has clean hands and a pure heart, Who has not lifted up his soul to an idol, Nor sworn deceitfully. He shall receive blessing from the LORD, And righteousness from the God of his salvation. (Psalms 24:4-5 NKJV)

Revelation

Everyone should desire daily revelation of the word of God but unfortunately most people don't get higher levels of revelation because they can't handle the truth over their preconceived ideas, nor can they choose to let go of a 'comfortable mentality'. Truth and Revelation are synonymous. You cannot have one without the other. Most often people get offended when they first hear truth because it goes against what they have set up as a belief system in their own heart. Truth will always reveal itself in time, so little seeds of truth are more important than you know when it comes to evangelism or even personal revelation. If too much truth is given at once, as much as it is beneficial, there will be a vast amount of pain. I liken it to pulling off a blind fold too quickly and briefly hurting the eyes in the process. There needs to be a process to perspective and in that process, we learn to desire more of God and not merely what He can give us. Revelation must be inherently multifaceted so that it can build upon itself for eternity, yet it must be so simple a child can understand it.

He told them another parable: "The Kingdom of Heaven is like a mustard seed, which a man took and planted in his field. Though it is the smallest of all seeds, yet when it grows, it is the largest of garden plants and becomes a tree, so that the birds come and perch in its branches. He told them still another parable: The Kingdom of Heaven is like yeast that a woman took and mixed into about sixty pounds of flour until it worked all through the dough. (Matthew 13:31-33 NIV)

If a child can't understand it and grasp the foundation of it, consider whose ideas and concepts you may be proclaiming? Did it show off how much you know and left the other person belittled? or did it edify everyone and bring others to a greater understanding into the heart of God. Jesus specifically said, *'let the children come to Him'* in Matthew 19:14, as the Kingdom of Heaven belongs to them. That means the functioning of the way of life from Heaven to Earth, must be able to be grasped as a child and not merely to the intellectual mind, so that we can come into the fullness of our true identity. It is to be caught with the spirit rather than the carnality of Earthly wisdom which is the knowledge of good and evil. There is no room for double mindedness or double standards for revelation. To function in revelation our intention needs to be for simplicity and purity sake regarding Heaven's culture.

Once we come to the spiritual truth that God presents on matters, should we then mix it with ideas we have learnt with human reasoning? That is not growing in revelation, that is mixture of the knowledge of good and evil and with the tree of life. We should eat only from the tree of life. As prophetic people we should know that the law of the spirit of life in Christ governs our spirit, soul and body. We ought to leave human reasoning behind and progress onto Godhood as sons of God. We will never manifest as sons of God until we are one track minded into the mind of God. If these concepts seem offensive, it is only because we as a body of Christ have not come to terms with our identity yet.

Functioning by the Spirit of Revelation is different to the ability to get revelation. How and why is this the case? Let's first question ourself to discover the differences. Do we have the desire to speak truth only? Are our thought patterns continually aligned with the desire for the truth? What are our heart's intentions for obtaining truth? - Is it to act like we know more than the next person and to be a person whose aim is to correct others, or do we have the desire for truth purely to delve deeper into the heart of God? Our motives gauge our ability to either function in revelatory knowledge as a means of who we are or opposingly receive revelation once in a blue moon from God to discipline and correct our motives. So one is the ability to function from the heart and mind of God, governed by a life lived in pursuit of truth from God alone, while the other is a loving disciplinary action from God to steer us back onto the right path. A son will get a loving rebuke by a loving father no matter where his focus lies. But we want to have a relationship with the Spirit of Revelation and Wisdom to direct our focus.

Faith

What is faith? It is confidence in God to remain true to who He is and to provide what you cannot see *yet* with your physical eyes but instead what you desire in your heart.

'Now faith is confidence in what we hope for and assurance about what we do not see.' (Hebrews 11:1 NIV)

To operate in that confidence in God, we need to choose to trust God over our natural reasoning. If you have noticed I have continually spoken about the carnal natured mind which we have become accustomed to using. The ability to reason was not given to you to talk yourself out of the truths of God, instead it was given to be able to discern the ways of God. Faith enables the realities of God and brings it into manifestation. Here's a quick story of using faith in the most peculiar of ways but I promise it's quite viable and reveals a simple attitude in the right direction of sonship.

When I was still at university, they used to set up stalls for orientation weeks. On a particular day having lunch with my girlfriend at the time. I saw a competition from a phone company to win a PlayStation 4 or a mobile phone. I said to my girlfriend while eating lunch 'Watch how much God loves me! I'm going to win a PlayStation for you.' She laughed, of course. So I put my name in the draw and I forgot about it. Lo and behold! a few weeks later I got a call saying I won the PlayStation and I won the phone as well! It was like an extra pat on the back. I called my girlfriend and told her 'See I told you my Daddy loves me'.

So did I need that? No, but God always confirms His word with signs and wonders. I ended up giving the PlayStation to her and the phone to my dad. Does it seem a little silly? You bet! But God is a Father first to us before being God. But in both aspects, He is love and all He requires is a little faith on our part. God desires to bless us exceedingly, abundantly, above and beyond all we can ever imagine or think (Ephesians 3:20). Maybe I think too foolishly to the carnal mind but I say we let Him bless us so we can be a blessing to others! Faith starts with a matter of changing your perspective. I've been blessed like this throughout my whole life and I will continue to be blessed in greater measures for all of eternity. Is that cockiness? Definitely not! It's faith/confidence that my Heavenly Father remains true to who He is. This way He gets the glory and I enjoy being a very, very loved son. You can have that too, just choose to start believing so.

'And without faith it is impossible to please God, because anyone who comes to him must believe that he exists and that he rewards those who earnestly seek him.' (Hebrews 11:6 NIV)

'Therefore I tell you, whatever you ask for in prayer, believe that you have received it, and it will be yours.' (Mark 11:24 NIV)

The Lord had given me a dream a while ago where I was required to stay in an apartment for a period of time. In the kitchen were 4 double doored fridges. In the dream I knew it was my Heavenly Father's fridges. They were packed full of every type of food including meat, vegetables and even ice cream in the freezers. I was given free access to eat and take as much as I desired. I won't tell you the rest of the dream because I want you to focus on the fact that God specifically showed me how He makes sure we have everything we need for the seasons of life we go through and it comes from Him. We may think it came from another person, but God is using that person to get it to you from Him. To enter into that season of my life required complete faith in God for myself. I could not provide for myself at all but every day He made sure I was taken care of with food, money, clothes, a roof over my head and resources to accomplish His will. I can't seem to separate enjoying a loving relationship and reliance upon God from faith. Faith may come from hearing and hearing the word of God (Romans 10:17) but it also grows through a life lived in reliance, surrender and trust in God.

What is the gift of faith? Simply an accelerated form of faith that bypassed the growing in faith stages. It is given based on desire and belief that it is attainable and that it is rightfully yours by inheritance. Spiritual gifts are given to encourage and build up the church in their confidence in God. Having this gift gives us complete understanding that God is good and truly is Almighty Sovereign God. Whatever God says goes, and there is no way out of reasoning from the voice of God for people who have this gift. They always wait on God and expect Him to show up in answer of a prayer or to perform miracles. Jesus said if we have faith as small as a mustard seed, we can move mountains in Matthew 17:20. Those with this gift do not care about the size of their faith, they care about living in the expectation of faith. The gift of faith also gives the ability to bypass any setbacks, meaning if for some reason a prayer is not answered the way we would like it to be or a healing/miracle does not happen, then the gift of faith allows the person to deal with every situation as if the last attempt was answered. Reality does not define truth, truth defines reality to these individuals. Even though reality or experience may not always submit to the truth of the word of God, their ability to stand in faith imparts faith for others to believe too.

Hope

Hope is a predetermined sense of security. Our ability to hope in the Lord comes from the ability that God cannot lie and has determined to bless us and our descendants. This is written on our hearts alongside His law. Having this security allows us as children of God to hold fast to 'the faith' that we profess. But what happens when we have lost hope? We have simply directed our eyes onto the external rather than maintain it on the internal. The inner man or the spirit is at continual rest in God and flooded with hope. The hope gateways are blocked by lack of clarity as to what the word of God says. The clearer and more streamlined our perspective and understanding of the word of God and His promises, the greater our ability to function with hope for life rather than death.

'Let us hold unswervingly to the hope we profess, for he who promised is faithful.' (Hebrews 10:23 NIV)

Where there is no hope, we begin to falter in our walk with God. This comes with confusion and the over emphasis on worldly activities. We are not called to be carnally minded.

'Hope deferred makes the heart sick, but a longing fulfilled is a tree of life.' (Proverbs 13:12 NIV)

Hope is indeed the anchor for our soul (Hebrews 6:19) and so without it we don't have a foothold to move forward with. If our longing(hope) does not get fulfilled, does that mean we have failed or believed a lie? On the contrary, hoping in God cannot make the heart sick for God renews those that wait upon Him. And the Lord will hear us if we wait patiently. What do we do if we are struggling with this aspect of our walk with God? We wait upon the Lord until He comes to our aid.

'But as for me, I watch in hope for the Lord, I wait for God my Saviour; my God will hear me'. (Micah 7:7 NIV)

'But those who wait on the Lord shall renew their strength; They shall mount up with wings like eagles, they shall run and not be weary, they shall walk and not faint.' (Isaiah 40:31 NKJV)

And so what is the point of hope? It is to bring glory to God not for selfish gain. Most hope for the best outcomes of life for themselves because that is how the world has led their minds to believe. No, the true hope has nothing to do with selfishness, in fact it is to bring the fullness of the body of Christ into perfection. With such a viewpoint we are able to grasp that Christ the hope of glory to God in us is to be manifested for the sake of encouraging one another to grow into all that Christ Jesus is. Something that never ceases to amaze me is the ability for God to continually encourage us through others or dreams and visions for ourselves or even through signs and wonders. When we see Heaven invade Earth, it is a consistent reassurance to those without hope. We therefore, especially in ministry, ought to remember that encouragement is a key component of the spiritual walk to bring hope to the body of Christ. It does not always have to be a fancy manifestation or prophetic word. It could be as simple as a hug. Love conquers all.

Worship

'Therefore, I urge you, brothers and sisters, in view of God's mercy, to offer your bodies as a living sacrifice, holy and pleasing to God--this is your true and proper worship. Do not conform to the pattern of this world, but be transformed by the renewing of your mind. Then you will be able to test and approve what God's will is--his good, pleasing and perfect will.' (Romans 12:1-2 NIV).

There is a place for praises and singing songs to enter into the presence of God. However, have you ever considered what the point of singing to God is? The Lord actually created a way for us to enter into His presence and then begin true worship. In times where the atmosphere is holy and we enter into an euphoric state, here we won't simply find words floating upwards to Heaven but instead an opening of ourselves in the form of portals to Heaven.

Worship is by no means singing a song. It is the giving of yourself over to God to receive all that God is into you. It is a taking on of His character and a putting off of the old self. When we begin to hand our bodies over to God to be used as His house, and to give ourselves over unto His holiness here we find that God delights Himself in us. A true expression of righteousness, peace and joy governed by the Holy Spirit. In this form of worship we give up our rights, our opinions and the way that seems right to a man which always leads to death. And we begin to have our carnal mind overpowered by the mind of Christ so that we may learn to love and have different thought processes and reasonings. The renewed mind manifests itself as we give our mind over to His mind. Once this occurs, we are able to know the will of God and understand His ways so that our ways mirror His, even to the point of knowing God's thoughts for others. It is always about love!

It is impossible then to be a prophetic person without worshiping in spirit and in truth (John 4:24). If prophecy is done outside of these dimensions, it falls prey to witchcraft or even lies and deception since it is not subject to the will of God. We must never try to be prophetic, but we should always aim to be in total surrender of God and abandon ourselves to Him for love's sake and then out of the overflow of the abundant supply of God's goodness, you will begin to manifest prophecy. It is in worship of our King that we find life and we begin to allow Heaven to invade this Earth. Worship then is the beginning of becoming one with God in divine union where you receive His blessings and become divine yourself. The healthiest, wealthiest and most successful people are true worshippers.

'Worship the Lord your God, and his blessing will be on your food and water. I will take away sickness from among you'. (Exodus 23:25 NIV).

With this in mind, the above verse means that we should become one with God to enjoy His provision, and to walk in divine health. We do not worship God to get Him to move for us, or in a manner of speaking - twist His arm to give us essential provisions. We worship God in adoration of who He is, and we present ourselves unto the will of God to personify all that He is. By default then, all that is yours is God's and all that is God's is yours. This is a true covenantal relationship.

Activation

Take the time to write out where you are at in your functioning of the spirit. The clearer our gateways are and the larger they become, the more readily we will be able to function within the prophetic from the ever proceeding voice of God.

Consider how your prophetic unction manifests and ask others how they feel they function as well. See how their life is managed by using that gateway realm to discern the prophetic. For example, if your one friend functions by gaining revelation, discover what that looks like in their life. If another functions by prayer, the fear of God or even worship, observe their highest functioning so that you can discover how each looks like. Then you will be able to have an anchor point for the type of functioning you can aim towards. Begin with the prayer and worship realms and watch how powerful prayer warriors pray and ask Holy Spirit to teach you to operate in a greater measure like they do. If it is prophetic worship, discover how they anticipate the prophetic nature through songs and lean towards the voice of God through worship.

Prayer

Lord help us to function and gain clear revelation of the prophetic. May we grow in insight and go beyond our giftings to function in completeness and wholeness as we begin to manifest as prophetic sons of God who are able to discern your voice and leading. May our prayer life, fear of God, reverence of God, intuition and knowing, revelatory abilities, faith levels, hopeful nature and ability to go deeper into worship of You God increase with all expectancy of fruitfulness. Help us to grow for both our sake and your people's sake. May we come to the full revelation that all prophetic abilities are grounded in love and may we function from love. May we grow into the fullness of Christ as our example and may we continue in holiness, purity and clean motives. In Jesus name, Amen!

9

A Prophet's Toolbox

Birthing Pains

I'd like to share something very personal only prophets will understand. This chapter won't be limited just for the sake of seers. If you are a prophet or you have an incredible prophetic call on your life, then I want you to know that you are not going through something strange or unique that others have not gone through. Taking up the prophetic call is not a choice because we are born prophets, chosen by God before coming to Earth. We have so many questions until we realise the truth of why we are so greatly dishonoured by the ones closest to us. I had no idea of the prophetic call on my life until I was at the age of 28. I knew stuff other people didn't, and I was so perplexed as to why they couldn't understand the things I used to say or why they had no grid to notice the things I noticed. In fact I was looked at as if I was doing something wrong for stating things to protect others even though it seemed so obvious to me but to others it seemed offensive, they were blinded, and it wasn't their fault. I dreamt continuously, I saw Jesus, Father God and Holy Spirit amongst other saints and angels in dreams, but it never crossed my mind that I could be a prophet. I was always wiser than all of my teachers, like David had made reference to, in Psalms 119, which is possible if we are grounded in the Word of God. I cared about Jesus and I was bold about it. It infuriated others, and because I didn't know anything about the call on my life, I tried to fit in with people but I was rejected or left out of groups at all points. I'm grateful now only because I understand who I am, but it wasn't easy holding my Bible and crying myself to sleep for years on end without anyone knowing. The pain a prophet has to go through cannot be explained. No matter how much you try, you are disregarded even though the Lord blesses you at all points because He protects His prophets. Even right now some readers may think I'm exaggerating but that also makes it clear that you have been blessed with a different calling. I'm saying it like that because many times I wished I didn't have to go through the things I've gone through only to function as a prophet. However, that pain of rejection has to be overcome and used as a tool to push you into a deeper relationship with God.

John 4:44 says 'Now Jesus himself had pointed out that a prophet has no honour in his own hometown.'

Most can never begin to understand how the devil uses a man's own family members, friends and acquaintances to show disrespect and force us to attempt to end our life to give up the prophetic call. The only reason I didn't commit suicide several times, was the fact that I didn't want to go to hell for taking my own life. I knew if I just held on even though life was so painful, I would at least be able to get to Heaven. That was my thought process anyways. Now I know that there is a grace for people who have committed suicide because they didn't want to kill the image of God in themselves, they just wanted the pain to stop. So don't fear if you have a family member or friend who took their own life, God truly is a loving God and understands that pain can be unbearable, especially if there is confusion and we don't know how to use it to go deeper into relationship with the Lord. In saying that, that should never be an option, because the love of Christ is far greater and knowing the truth, we would have no excuse! If I had ended my life, I would never have come to the realisation of how loved I am by God and I would never have had the chance to inspire others and teach them to represent Christ correctly.

Many things happened to reveal the prophetic call the Lord gave me, such as a ridiculous amount of signs and wonders as well as prophecies from several different sources. When I finally came to the understanding of the function I was given for ministry, it didn't come as a shock, more like a relief that the pain I went through made sense finally. Amazingly, Jesus heals everything and pours out love that is far stronger than death. But I believe that pain was the biggest tool to push me into a deeper relationship and desire for Jesus more than anything else! Would I have chosen otherwise now? Even though my flesh would cry out wishing it didn't have to be a painful process, my spirit says, 'To live is Christ, to die is gain' and I would not have it any other way! Nor should you. Your destiny is far too great for what would be compared to as a small amount of pain for 30 years. Eternity is FOREVER! Jesus means more than anything to a prophet and nothing can by any means separate us from the love of Christ. I hope in sharing that, that those who are called to be prophets reading this book will have encouragement that there is light at the end of the tunnel and the present sufferings fail in comparison to the glory of God that will be revealed in us. Honour awaits but humility comes before honour (Proverbs 15:33). Always use pain as a driving force to propel you into the arms of our loving Heavenly Father. There will be many trying times and seasons of hiddenness until the Lord reveals you to the public eye and gives you the honour that is due unto you.

Fasting

As I was growing up, I was taught incorrectly about fasting. Religion always makes you have to do something to get God to move. It's absolutely devastating, because the truth is it's the doctrines of demons. We cannot do anything more to force or twist God's arm to get something from Him. We need to realise that God is continually giving, and we need to be rested in Him to be continually receiving. But that's easier said than done. Unbelief is not merely the absence of belief. Unbelief comes through circumstances of life that do not go our way and makes us blame God as if He is to blame, but He is not to blame at all. He is the answer to our life's problems. It is our own strongholds of unbelief that have set itself up to reject the power and oversupply of God in our life. Yes, you are so powerful that you can reject God. That is where fasting comes in. Fasting was given to us as a tool to remove patterns of unbelief. The word of God is full of references to the saints spending time in prayer and fasting. These two components if done together through a lifestyle of ongoing periods of fasting unlocks our full potential as divine beings joined in unity with Christ.

What happens when we fast? Our spiritual capacity grows. The reliance upon food diminishes as your reliance upon God increases. Fasting in the Bible is always to do with food. A very sad reality is that modern mainstream churches have said things along the lines of fasting social media, or tv is fine. That is not fasting. That's a discipline issue and I apologise if you have been taught incorrectly but the Lord is calling us into the truth of the word of God and we ought to dive into greater truths by understanding why fasting food is essential. The reactions of the body by giving up food are unparalleled to anything else. It is an impossibility for you to feel the same aches, pains and spiritual receptivity and freedom from the addiction or/reliance upon a fundamental bodily need by doing anything other than giving up certain foods. Your receptivity to the voice of God cannot increase without the removal of other voices in your life or idols upon the altar of your heart. Now of course if the Lord soverignly chooses you to fast something unrelated to food that may be because He is removing your dependence upon that thing, whatever it may be.

Fasting is the biggest tool we have to come against patterns of unbelief and selfishness, in fact it automatically removes it as we submit to fasting and prayer. It puts diligence inside of you and makes you adamant of the belief you are aiming for. Fasting is a tool used to break us free from the bondage of slavery and harmful effects of the carnal nature. It will expand your spirit's capacity and give you an ease to living from the spirit instead.

'Is not this the kind of fasting I have chosen: to loose the chains of injustice and untie the cords of the yoke, to set the oppressed free and break every yoke?' (Isaiah 58:6 NIV)

We can also expect different results for different types of fasting. I am sure there are more types of fasts, but the primary types are water only, Daniel fast 1 (vegetables and water), Daniel fast 2 (no pleasant food, no meat, no wine and no application of lotions/oils to the body) and finally a dry fast. If the Lord leads you differently, that is your own personal conviction and I am sure the Lord has His reasons for it. Trust Him and the process of the fast He calls you into. As the saints fasted in the bible, we should do the same and likewise we should expect the same results! Jesus is always our example; I don't understand why we think we can expect results like Him if we aren't willing to follow Him fully, especially in fasting! There was never an 'if you fast' but a 'when you fast' mentality. We as prophetic people should aim to live a lifestyle of fasting. I would like to draw our attention to a water fast used to unlock power and remove unbelief; and the 10 day Daniel fast used to unlock revelation, knowledge and understanding especially pertaining to dreams and visions! The 2nd form of Daniel fast for 21 days was used in mourning by Daniel as He needed clarity on a very disturbing prophecy of the end times. I believe we are close to those days that he saw – a topic for another book.

When Jesus entered the desert and fasted for 40 days, He did not have food. Whether He had water or not is unclear, but I don't think it was relevant for the first accusation the devil used to test him, which was tempting Him to turn the stone into bread (A symbol of getting eternal life from following the law rather than living by relationship with God, conveyed by His response which is to live by the ever proceeding word of God. (Matthew 4:4)). Once Jesus had finished the 40 days of fasting, He came out of the desert filled with the power of the Spirit.

'Then Jesus returned in the power of the Spirit to Galilee, and news of Him went out through all the surrounding region' (Luke 4:14 NKJV).

This fast of 40 days gives us power and adamancy, it should be done in isolation if possible because the devil is cunning, and he will test you! We should not be afraid that the devil will try to test us though, especially on extended fasts. He will use anyone he can to try and stop you. Hold your ground and focus on the reason why you are fasting or go into isolation like Jesus did so people can't look upon you to question you or put their opinions on you. Your body will get very thin even though you may feel like you can run a marathon! Fasting is between you and God. During that time your body really is functioning by the power of the Spirit and you are living purely by the daily word and instruction of the Lord. It is never a condemning thing if you do not make the full length of days. Fasting is a tool for your own sake and not God's as I said previously. But if God leads you to specifically fast a certain number of days, He will give you the grace for it, to empower you.

What is the significance of 40 days? In Hebrew the number 10 coincides with the alphabet letter *Yod*, which pictographically is represented by a hand or the hand of God. The number 4 is *Dalet* pictographically represented as a Doorway. Combining the 4x10 we are able to get the concept that 'the Hand of God opens the door'. These open doors are opportunities for your destiny from God! Finally we also have 40 which is represented by the letter *Mem*. Pictographically *Mem* is shown as water/chaos. All prophetic people know that living water is representative of Holy Spirit. So in combination of all these elements the 40 day fast symbolically represents God opening the doors for ministering through the power of the Holy Spirit. And what happened with Jesus after 40 days? Jesus came out of the desert with the power of the Spirit. These *Numerology* and *Gematria* truths are hiding and scattered in every verse of the bible! It's God's fingerprint to reveal truth to those that seek it. God is the master of hiding secrets for His children to find!

The Daniel fast is for a very specific outcome. I like to use this fast to get smarter and healthier. Seriously! Shadrach, Meshach, Abednego and Daniel chose not to eat the choice foods from the King because it went against the traditional laws of the Jews. So they ate only vegetables and drank water for 10 days and received knowledge and understanding from the hand of God! This is especially useful for prophets to understand visions and receive greater ability to interpret dreams.

'Please test your servants for ten days: Give us nothing but vegetables to eat and water to drink' (Daniel 1:12 NIV)

'At the end of the ten days they looked healthier and better nourished than any of the young men who ate the royal food' (Daniel 1:15 NIV).

'To these four young men God gave knowledge and understanding of all kinds of literature and learning. And Daniel could understand visions and dreams of all kinds' (Daniel 1:17 NIV).

What's really amazing to me is that there were none equal to them! And were found to be 10 times smarter! Now we know from the Gematria explanation above that it actually means that their knowledge and understanding was influenced by the hand of God.

'The king talked with them, and he found none equal to Daniel, Hananiah, Mishael and Azariah; so they entered the king's service. In every matter of wisdom and understanding about which the king questioned them, he found them

ten times better than all the magicians and enchanters in his whole Kingdom'. (Daniel 1:19-20 NIV)

Wouldn't you like to be that smart? Definitely so! I've noticed that fasting and prayer is tied to humility and rightfully so since it is not fitting that we should be wise in our own eyes and let pride come in only to be cast out of Heaven as satan was.

Tongues

The power of life and death are in your tongue! (Proverbs 18:21) Often we know not what to pray for and so the ability to pray in unknown tongues allows our spirit to pray and to groan deep within ourselves of which our natural speech and natural mind cannot articulate. The use of tongues is so multifaceted that it really is the precursor to moving and walking in the Spirit. There is no point to anything of the spirit if it does not affect the soul and the body. We are called into oneness as God is one and then oneness in God. Every person is made in the image of God, if love is our motive then no foul language should come out of our mouth. Not even crude joking.

'But no man can tame the tongue. It is an unruly evil, full of deadly poison.' (James 3:8 NKJV)

Only the spiritual man of God can tame the tongue because he is no longer a mere man, he is a son of God with the ability to speak life only as He mirrors the Father. Tongues give us the ability to override our carnal tongue, the more you do it, the more ability you have to speak according to the Spirit and manifest the power of life.

Tongues remove selfish prayer. When we pray with our natural mind, we tend to pick and choose our words and the prayer becomes biased for our own good unless we purposefully intercede for another.

Tongues allow us to pray in unity as one spirit, the desires of the spirit. There are no hidden agendas or false motives when praying in the spirit.

Tongues is an exceptional tool to renew the mind according to the Spirit so that we do not conform to the mindsets of others or the carnal nature. In fact we as a new creation need to come to the realisation that we don't have sin inside of us any longer. That is no longer who we are. The ability to sin does not make us sinners nor does it mean that there is sin in you. As Christ is so are you (1 John 4:17). Otherwise Jesus died for nothing, but He became sin itself and was nailed to a cross, the same way the serpent was, which was attacking the Jews in the desert during Moses' day. As they looked upon it, they were redeemed from that which was killing them. The same with looking at sin on the cross which was taken upon the body of Christ. Such a concept is caught with the spirit and needs to come forth to the soul and our body. Tongues can be used therefore to pray for the renewing of the soul through the truth of the spirit and overflowing into the body and out through our motives and actions. This way we allow the mind of Christ which is already ours to have free reign over our own mind and in doing so we begin to have God's mind for others.

'For "who has known the mind of the LORD that he may instruct Him?" But we have the mind of Christ'. (1 Corinthians 2:16 NKJV).

This is a powerful concept to come to terms with since words of knowledge and prophecy can easily come from being under subjection to the mind of Christ. Of course, love must be our governing force or else we will enter into pride and operating under a spiritual gift rather than letting our motive be for recognising the created value of a man made in the image of God.

Continually praying in tongues helps us to stay conscious of the presence of Holy Spirit and in consistent communication with Holy Spirit. In doing this we begin to be led by the spirit and we enter into making correct decisions by the spirit. Logical decisions made by the natural mind which is governed by the knowledge of good and evil, are overruled as I explained previously. Instead we gain the ability to make firm decisions based on eating from the tree of life. The path becomes narrow and confusion is displaced by the perfect will of God. And we can pray for the perfect plan of God for our lives, our families and even people we may have never even met yet. Praying in tongues is not limited to the present but the same way we pray for future events, allowing the spirit to lead us, can guide us to pray for future events that we don't even know is coming! And we can trust that it is good since it comes from producing the fruit of the spirit and not what is contrary to it.

'But the fruit of the Spirit is love, joy, peace, forbearance, kindness, goodness, faithfulness, gentleness and self-control. Against such things there is no law.' (Galatians 5:22-23 NIV).

Tongues can be used for all things! It refreshes your spirit and brings the soul under subjection of the peace of God. Often if a situation came as a shock I would immediately pray in tongues and the peace of God that surpasses all understanding would overtake me. It builds faith by stirring the spirit within us.

Often, we have no idea how to come against matters of spiritual warfare, so speaking in tongues becomes our sword as we proclaim the word of God in unknown tongues. There have been several nights that I would get attacked in the middle of the night by demons. Our perceptions in the spirit are acute while we are asleep and in the in-between phase of sleeping and waking. I have awoken screaming in tongues from fighting demons in my dreams, and even casting out demons. Understanding your authority in conjunction with speaking in tongues is equal to the life-giving power of God's word in His own mouth! It is indeed forceful power when it needs to be.

'And these signs will accompany those who believe: In my name they will drive out demons; they will speak in new tongues...' (Mark 16:17 NIV)

Finally, it aids in praise and in worship since our natural tongue is so limited in its ability to convey emotion. Tongues especially used in singing allows us to grasp heights that are only reachable by entering through worship in the spirit and in truth!

'For anyone who speaks in a tongue[a] does not speak to people but to God. Indeed, no one understands them; they utter mysteries by the Spirit'. (1 Corinthians 14:2 NIV).

This is a secret on tongues that I use every day. Pray in tongues as you fall asleep. You will notice that you may wake yourself up from hearing yourself still praying in tongues while asleep. But you will end up dreaming more, and hearing God's voice clearer throughout the night. It is not limited to only discipline or rebuke. The Lord may take you in the spirit and accomplish Kingdom business while you are still asleep.

'In a dream, in a vision of the night, when deep sleep falls on people as they slumber in their beds, he may speak in their ears and terrify them with warnings, to turn them from wrongdoing and keep them from pride, to preserve them from the pit, their lives from perishing by the sword.' (Job 33:15-16 NIV)

I have heard many stories of people praying for others in hospital, yet they were asleep in bed at the time. But they got a text message or a call thanking them the next day for coming to visit the sick person.

On one occasion an extremely peculiar thing happened! My girlfriend had a dream in her own home being chased by someone and I in my own home dreamt at the exact same time that I began fighting with some guy who went to attack her and pushed him over while praying in tongues. When I called her on the phone in the morning and heard her version of the story, I was shocked. How was I finishing off her dream? I believe our dreams are more about spiritual activity than we realise. If angels can appear to us to warn us in a dream, like in Joseph's case as he ran away with Mary and Jesus from King Herod, that would also mean that God sent that angel to interact with him by the spirit to lead him (Matthew 2:13). Tongues are powerful and it allows you to do things that you didn't think were possible or even know about. I have a personal conviction which may or may not be true. But if it is true, it would explain quite a few things! According to science we only use roughly 10% of our brain. I believe the other 90% has to do with the things of the spirit. We also just so happen to have nine spiritual gifts that correspond and allow us to operate with supernatural abilities which we don't usually have. Just a thought to leave you with but may in fact be truer than we can imagine.

Hanging Out With Other Prophets

Prophets should try to associate themselves with other prophets and form a group of close-knit friends. Often, we can neglect relationships simply to be with the Lord as intercessors, but that is not our calling to be hidden, unless that is a specific instruction you have received from the Lord for a time. In fact, it is quite the opposite, we are called to lead others and provide direction for people's lives. Being able to impart spiritual gifts and receive words from God for others and the church is our speciality. We should be the most advanced innovators in all areas of life as we are also called to be forerunners of the Heavenly culture.

Forming a prophetic community will allow your prophetic abilities to sharpen even to the point of allowing the Spirit of the Lord to overtake you and be transformed into a new person. This happened with Saul. He was not a prophet. However, he was given the ability when the Spirit of God came upon Him and He began to prophesy along with the other prophets.

'When they came there to the hill, there was a group of prophets to meet him; then the Spirit of God came upon him, and he prophesied among them. And it happened, when all who knew him formerly saw that he indeed prophesied among the prophets, that the people said to one another, "What is this that has come upon the son of Kish? Is Saul also among the prophets? And when he had finished prophesying, he went to the high place.' (1 Samuel 10:10-12 NKJV)

The Lord will always hide His prophets for a season before releasing them to the public. During that time they are to learn to enter the high places of the Lord to receive revelation so that they are able to minister in the future. We never grow in front of the prophetic groups we involve ourselves in, we always grow behind closed doors alone with the Lord. The prophetic flow is only heightened amongst other prophets because the spirit of the Lord forms an arc between the people and the presence of the Lord is usually experienced in greater measure to release the built up prophetic abilities that have been received in the secret place. Prophets then, who meet together should take turns and let onlookers judge the prophecy for the sake of peace and unity. The unity of the spirits' of prophets should demonstrate the will of God. Remember prophecy is for the edification of one another, therefore love must be at the forefront and the desire for truth and the perfect will of God. It should also be used to teach others how to do the same. All may prophesy, however the motive behind the need to prophecy needs to be judged and weighed against other prophecies.

Let two or three prophets speak, and let the others judge. But if anything is revealed to another who sits by, let the first keep silent. For you can all prophesy one by one, that all may learn and all may be encouraged. And the spirits of the prophets are subject to the prophets. For God is not the author of confusion but of peace, as in all the churches of the saints (1 Corinthians 14:29-33 NKJV).

Because everyone is still growing in the area of love, it is so essential to be alert and protect your heart. Prophets are very sensitive because of their ability to receive from God. If pain or rejection comes from anyone, especially people that respect has been given to, it needs to be dealt with as it can hinder the prophetic flow. Never take gathering with other prophetic individuals or believers as a replacement for your own alone time with God. Nothing can replace that. When God is sought in secret, your Heavenly Father will reward you.

Activation

Take time to fast by asking the Lord how He would like you to fast and which type of fasting is necessary for your walk with the Lord. Ask for grace to empower you to complete the fasts that you choose to embark on. And make the decision to fast regularly so that you can remain sharp as a prophet. Tongues should never be neglected, it should be done much more than we speak in our mother tongue, as Paul says, that He spoke in tongues more than all of them (1 Corinthians 14:18). Speaking in tongues will allow you to keep yourself conscious of the Holy Spirit and your walk with the Lord will result in less mistakes as you begin to perceive the voice of the Lord more readily.

If you have prophetic friends, speak to them often and ask what the Lord is speaking to them about currently or have told/taught them recently. Doing this will stir your spirit so that the spirit of prophecy will continually be stirred as you bear witness to the works of the Lord.

Finally, whether you have been placed in the office of a prophet or merely growing in the prophetic and have suffered a great deal because of it, be sure to forgive anyone that has rejected you or become a stumbling block to you. Love is the goal of our instruction and the prophetic flow can be hindered by our own ability to hold onto hurt in our soul.

Prayer

Father give me the grace to grow in the prophetic. Thank You for the tools *that You have given me to grow in the prophetic and to use to gain revelation. Help me to have the discipline to fast and to pray in tongues often. Please put Godly, prophetic people with clean motives and a pure heart in my life to associate with that I may have friendship and companionship to run the race that has been marked out before me. May no one, or anything ever take your place as my first true love. Thank You that You are my comforter, deliverer and ever-present help in time of need. May I use these tools not in a boastful manner but do all things without ulterior motives, but instead with clean hands and a pure heart as I delve into a greater relationship with you. I ask in Jesus name, Amen!*

10

Engaging The Secret Place

This is the birthing place of destiny! This is the simplest thing we could ever do and yet people continue to over complicate it. If I told you it's easier than breathing yet harder than the issues of life would you believe it? Why is it easier than breathing? Because that is literally what you need to do, simply turn your attention to Jesus and be in complete stillness and adoration of Jesus and simply be still. On the other hand, why is it so hard? Because it requires you to stop what you are doing and turn your focus onto Jesus. With the hustle and bustle of life and the to dos of everyday life it can be extremely hard to find a moment free from the noise of people and workload to look at Jesus and just breathe. We see such a beautiful picture of what this looks like from Mary and Martha.

Now it happened as they went that He entered a certain village; and a certain woman named Martha welcomed Him into her house. And she had a sister called Mary, who also sat at Jesus' feet and heard His word. But Martha was distracted with much serving, and she approached Him and said, "Lord, do You not care that my sister has left me to serve alone? Therefore tell her to help me." And Jesus answered and said to her, "Martha, Martha, you are wor-

ried and troubled about many things. But one thing is needed, and Mary has chosen that good part, which will not be taken away from her." (Luke 10:38-42 NKJV)

If we study through the scriptures, we see that Mary was at every place that she needed to be at, at the right time. She was at the foot of the cross and at the tomb as the one to see Jesus first, amongst other key moments. I bet her infatuation with Jesus led her to always being present at the right moment in time for the purposes of the Lord. We can have the same occurrences in our life, being able to be at the right place at the right time. But how do we make that happen? Simply behold Jesus. Consider being attentive to His voice and presence continually in your life! What does that look like practically? Since I'm normally working at the computer and half the time, I have no clue what I'm doing, I simply stop doing whatever I'm doing, close my eyes, take a deep breath, lift my hands slightly and say, 'Jesus I worship You'. In that moment, peace, righteousness and joy begin entering, and as I feel myself getting filled up with that internal bliss then I continue about my work. Sometimes it could be as simple as entering into that posture and asking, 'God what am I meant to do here' and then just listen for a moment and don't reject the gentle internal whisper from the Holy Spirit. He always speaks. Simple right? Try it! and you will become addicted to it! The presence of the Lord will not depart, and you will continue to abide in Him as He is in you.

'Whoever dwells in the shelter of the Most High will rest in the shadow of the Almighty. I will say of the Lord, "He is my refuge and my fortress, my God, in whom I trust."' (Psalm 91:1-2 NIV)

I suggest taking time to often read through Psalm 91, it is filled with tonnes of revelation and draws you into such deep intimacy with God. The shelter of the Most High is the ultimate protection, and the ability to rest in the shadow of the Almighty demonstrates to us the extent of the power of God so that we have nothing to fear as we choose to rest in His presence. Indeed, we can trust that Almighty God has the power over all of your life circumstances, so that nothing can harm you. Letting go and letting God take over can be very scary unless you have developed a life of surrendering to him. As you engage the presence of God regularly with the expectation of the presence of God, it will increase your receptivity to His voice and presence, and you will begin to have visions and hear things in the spirit. Manifestations from Heaven are sure to follow!

True Prayer by the Spirit

As I touched on in the previous chapter, the Lord sees us in the secret place, and He rewards us for seeking Him when no one else is looking. That doesn't mean He doesn't see you throughout the day. He loves you way too much to ever take His eyes off you! His reward is Himself, and with Him comes Heaven's blessings which includes everything you need in this life!

'But when you pray, go into your room, close the door and pray to your Father, who is unseen. Then your Father, who sees what is done in secret, will reward you.' (Matthew 6:6 NIV).

So when we pray, we should go into our inner room and close the door. Why is that necessary? Let's look at that from the flesh. We could go into our bedroom and close the door behind us so we can be alone with Jesus. Right? What if you can't do that? Many people across the world don't have the opportunity to be alone. Most people are married or share bedrooms with their siblings. So there must be a deeper spiritual aspect. Here's the spiritual aspect. Going into your inner room is symbolic of entering into the Holy of Holies by engaging your own spirit and then closing the door symbolises shutting off the noise, voices and thoughts of your daily life from clouding your mind. Our attention being solely focused on Jesus changes from the body to the soul and to the spirit. In each phase of praying, the way we speak changes automatically. Let's explore what that looks like by noticing key practical truths to begin practicing.

'Ask and it will be given to you; seek and you will find; knock and the door will be opened to you. For everyone who asks receives; the one who seeks finds; and to the one who knocks, the door will be opened. (Matthew 7:8 NIV)

There are multiple levels of revelation from this verse. This verse is not merely about asking God for something, then seeking after it and then being persistent with God until you get it. This has to do with the phases of prayer that we go through, body to soul to spirit, outer court to inner court (Holy place) to the Holy of Holies. Remember your body is the temple of the Holy Spirit (1 Corinthians 6:19). This is similar for praise and worship but for now I will explain the instances of prayer realms.

'Still other seed fell on good soil, where it produced a crop—a hundred, sixty or thirty times what was sown.' (Matthew 13:8 NIV)

Outer Court, Body, Ask Realm

You can liken this area to the 30-fold blessing. We usually start in the body asking God for things, 'please bless so and so, I need this, please provide this, this and this' etc. Here we are in the Outer Court which is the first phase of prayer. In the Outer Court our fleshly nature is to be crucified. It is a parallel to the need for cleansing and atonement by the sacrifices done with bulls and goats, but of course we accept the sacrifice of Jesus now, so technically since He has done it once for all, we should never have to live from this realm or the soul realm but only in the spirit since His blood forever cries forgiveness and goes up as incense continually forever. The Outer Court mentality is a very carnal minded experience and we will often continue to find comfortability in our posturing, either scratching our nose or face, or being distracted by any noise or even struggling to find the words to say etc. Sound familiar? We should be giving praise, respect and honour to God as we begin entering into His courts. Some people stop here. They never enter into the next phase. People who have not developed their prayer life don't stay long enough to enter into the next phase. These people continually fall prey to doing something to try to get God to move.

Inner Court, Soul, Seek Realm

You may liken this realm to the 60-fold blessing. As we continue in prayer, after about 10-15 mins we crossover into the seeking realm, the soul and the inner court of the temple. Our prayers and worship here go up as incense before God. It is symbolic of Jesus' body and blood as our sacrifice producing the fragrant aroma that is similar to the unleavened bread and meat that was poured on the rock (Christ).

'The Angel of God said to him, "Take the meat and the unleavened bread and lay them on this rock, and pour out the broth." And he did so. Then the Angel of the LORD put out the end of the staff that was in His hand, and touched the meat and the unleavened bread; and fire rose out of the rock and consumed the meat and the unleavened bread. And the Angel of the LORD departed out of his sight.' (Judges 6:20-21 NKJV)

Our language, prayer and petition changes into thanksgiving. This happens automatically as our attention remains on God. We are not so easily distracted, and we often start crying around here as we recognise the goodness of God. The presence of God is usually starting to be felt here as well, your experience changes and the Kingdom of God: Righteousness, Peace and Joy starts to manifest itself. We should be focused on this and not the outward feeling of goosebumps, that's just a by-product of reacting to the presence of God (His frequency).

If we ask anything here, we normally begin speaking with a mentality of 'Your will be done, not mine'. We go a step further and we start asking God 'what would You like me to pray for'. Does this all sound familiar? This faith realm requires us to exercise our authority, by speaking at the mountains or situations of our life and commanding them to move. Most Christians who have a prayer life stop here and they operate in the area of faith. Unfortunately, there is normally a mixture between the next phase of simple belief and faith because people don't realise that faith requires a strong soul but believing requires simple being.

Good well-meaning Christians who desperately pursue God often get stuck in this faith realm because they don't realise there is more. They operate under the law of faith and it is because they only ever get to this phase in prayer. The mainstream churches always stop here! They never allow people to enter into the fullness of the Kingdom and they refuse to enter themselves. Jesus was furious at the religious leaders of His day for doing this.

'But woe to you, scribes and Pharisees, hypocrites! For you shut up the Kingdom of Heaven against men; for you neither go in yourselves, nor do you allow those who are entering to go in.' (Matthew 23:13 NKJV)

Holy of Holies, Spirit, Knock Realm

After about 45 mins to an hour (or less depending on how seasoned you are) we cross into the spirit realm. Here we operate under the law of the Spirit of Life in Christ. This is something they do not teach you often in churches, so people are always left trying to figure things out in their own strength, and getting by in life without any power, prophetic ability or becoming love. If they do have any it is because they have nurtured a strong soul and mostly operate from 'faith' rather than from 'being'. And they never get transformed, obtain the mind of Christ or get transfigured like Jesus did. Here we enter into 'the rest' of God and we allow God to actually be God of our lives. True surrender, intimacy and oneness of spirit occurs here.

Here's an example. Either our confession is, 'Jesus please heal me' – 30-fold, 'body be healed in Jesus name' – 60-fold or 'I am healing, as Christ is so am I in this world, if He lives in me then I already am 'the healed' of the Lord. I have life, healing and all I need by the Spirit of God in me' – 100-fold. Can you see the distinction in belief systems? To enter into this mentality and begin operating our lives from the 100-fold blessing we need to continually abide in the Spirit. So in prayer we go from body to soul to spirit. This realm requires us to be extremely still to enter into. Getting up to go get a glass of water here will set you back and you will need to start again.

'Be still, and know that I am God; I will be exalted among the nations, I will be exalted in the Earth.' (Psalm 46:10 NKJV)

As you cross over into the spirit, there is no more talking. Remember this is automatic, you are not just trying not to talk. You just can't! because of the euphoric state of being one with God in that moment. If there are any thoughts you have here, they are answered instantly by God. Our soul unfortunately is used to being subject to our body so that the soul lingers with the body instead of travelling with the spirit and receiving information that way. It takes years of persistence of prayer by the spirit to make your soul subject to your spirit. Therefore we see glimpses of the spiritual realm. We may think we have fallen asleep but when you come out of the spirit you don't feel like you slept, you feel like you were not here on Earth, like you were somewhere else and you just want to go back to wherever you were so much! You were most likely in Heaven with God. But you come back to consciousness wishing you didn't have to face reality, because that sweet serenity takes you into such an euphoric, blissful state. In this state, your spirit is one with God and it begins to override your soul and body. True worship and true prayer begin here and petitioning by the Spirit of God occurs. Deep desires of your heart that are according to the will of God are prayed for and answered in this place. It's impossible for you to open your mouth to utter anything in this place because you have checked out of your body, your spiritual senses have become golden. You will often receive visions, thoughts or voices from God which you know are not your own, and you will become acutely aware of the presence of God. Your body goes numb, your breathing slows down and your heart rate drops. I have heard stories where some people have died in this place and when their spirit comes back into their body, they are alive again. Paul said that to be absent from the body is to be present with the Lord. This is the place where that is developed (2 Corinthians 5:8).

Often when I have been in the spirit, if any noise is made my body gets a scary shock! My body reacts completely differently than it would if I were asleep. My heart pounds hard and fast, I begin gasping for air and my chest hurts until I am able to calm down again which may be after several minutes. Even the vibration of my phone could possibly jolt my heart to begin pounding in my chest. It's not a nice feeling coming back into your body like that. It is absolutely imperative that you isolate yourself for this, because you are going up, into the mountain of God and communicating with God, spirit to spirit, exactly as Moses and Jesus did on their respective mountain top experiences. You are being purified by the glory of God and transfiguration is taking place. People who continually enter into the spirit have the greatest of signs, wonders, manifestations and anointing on their life. They have true authentic power in their life. More importantly they do not need to try to love, the Kingdom of God: righteousness, peace and joy overtakes them and becomes one with them as their spirit and Holy Spirit becomes one. As we yield to God in this place we become like God and become one. There is no more trying for you in life. Every step you take their after is ordained by God. You can take one step and be thousands of steps ahead of everyone else in life. A true 'Mary lifestyle' is born in this place, and the busyness of the 'Martha way of life' in us, dies! Prayer becomes simple, a deeper desire for God fills your heart. You can't help but desire to pull yourself away continually to be alone with the Lord anymore. This is why we see Jesus continually going to be alone praying on the mountain.

'I am the door. If anyone enters by Me, he will be saved, and will go in and out and find pasture. The thief does not come except to steal, and to kill, and to destroy. I have come that they may have life, and that they may have it more abundantly.' (John 10:9-10 NKJV)

Our attention must be on Jesus and Holy Spirit must lead us through the body of Jesus to enter into the Holy of Holies. His body was the veil or curtain that was torn so that we could all have access into the Holy of Holies and not only the High Priest (Matthew 27:51, Hebrews 9:7). If we do not enter through Jesus Christ, through the narrow path, we open ourselves up to demons as we enter into the spirit realms by other means. The way to destruction is broad! (Matthew 7:13-14). All drugs, all forms of smoking, psychedelics, other idol worship, things such as yoga, chanting and meditation, and anything else there may be which is not under subjection of Jesus can open up the spiritual gateways and allow demons to enter. This is especially important for prayer and waiting on God in stillness. Anything that you begin to rely on to the point of addiction or not being able to function without it becomes your god as you have submitted yourself to it rather than allowing God to be your source and oversupply of life.

Can your spirit be doing something else while your body and soul are conscious? Yes, but that may only happen if you were not originally in a state of prayer. God can divinely cause your spirit to do something while your body goes along even speaking by itself. To get to a position where your soul goes with your spirit while your body goes on autopilot, takes years of a life lived in the spirit with God, unless God sovereignly chooses to do it for His own reasons. However, prayer is where you learn to commune with God and become one with Him first, we should never chase after these experiences without God leading us.

Waiting on God

The western world perverted the idea of waiting on God by going about life and colloquially using the term 'I'm just waiting on God for my miracle brother'. This is not what is meant by waiting on God!

'Son of man, I have made you a watchman for the people of Israel; so hear the word I speak and give them warning from me.' (Ezekiel 33:7 NIV)

A real prayer life for me only started when I began to wake before the sun. During the 4th watch of the night from 3am – 6am is the quietest point of the day. It is completely still and the spiritual activity in the atmosphere is at its peak! Most often people dream around this time, angelic visitations happen, and your ability to hear God is much clearer as all of your spiritual senses are heightened. This is the best time to get up to pray and wait on the Lord. Jesus is our perfect example who did this regularly.

Now in the morning, having risen a long while before daylight, He went out and departed to a solitary place; and there He prayed. (Mark 1:35 NKJV)

Waiting on God is the most important thing we can do. We babble on talking, asking for things even begging, when we could easily come to the end of ourselves quickly and begin listening for the Lord to speak. When we wait on the Lord we manifest the Kingdom of God: righteousness, peace and joy in the Holy Spirit. The presence of God becomes tangible and we will regain lost strength and ability in our walk with the Lord. The point of waiting on God is to enter into the Spirit and to hear from Him. When we approach God like this, humility is absolutely vital because Holy Spirit will never turn anyone away unless they come full of themselves. When we wait in stillness, patience and humility, we are able to truly wait and begin to receive directly from the heart of God to ours.

'But those who wait on the Lord Shall renew their strength; They shall mount up with wings like eagles, They shall run and not be weary, They shall walk and not faint. (Isaiah 40:31 NKJV)

Teaching Dreams On Kingdom Prayer

I received two dreams where the Lord taught me how to pray and wait upon Him. If I didn't have these dreams I would never have learnt how to wait on God or pray in the secret place with Jesus. I desperately desire each of you reading this to begin to have dreams and visions where the Lord Himself will teach you, if not send you saints or angels to teach you as well. No one starts off fully matured, but they can be taught correctly, put on the right path and given impartation to help the journey.

In the first dream I followed Jesus down a flight of stairs into what I thought was a wine cellar. Instead it was a dead end with three blank walls. I then saw Jesus kneel down and begin crawling through a small hole in the wall. I followed in after Him. We sat down together on a seat by the wall. Jesus looked over at another guy that was there facing the other wall and seemed to be voiding himself of all thoughts, emotions and trying to be alone. Jesus looked at me, laughed and said, 'I don't know what that guy is doing'. That was the end of the dream. It was so full of symbolism and meaning! It showed me exactly what I need to do about entering into the secret place with the Most High God. As Jesus knelt down and crawled through into the small area it showed me that we must approach with humility and indeed it is the narrow path! We need to be following Jesus as I did in the dream. It was also a wine cellar that we entered into, which speaks of the new covenant that we are in with Jesus.

'I have set the LORD always before me; Because He is at my right hand I shall not be moved.' (Psalm 16:8 NKJV)

When we get into the secret place our attention needs to be fully on Jesus unlike the man who was becoming blank and empty, facing the wall. And finally Jesus laughing with me, made me realise that we are just meant to enjoy Him! I bet you could probably get tonnes of more revelation out of this dream, but these were the key things for me.

In the 2nd dream, I was in a place that looked something like the hidden Elf paradise from the Lord of the Rings. The backdrop was of the beautiful waterfalls and buildings in the mountain ranges. It was night, and the atmosphere was spiritually charged with God's presence! Eric Gilmour stood at a pulpit by the balcony and faced a crowd of people that I was a part of. We broke into groups of 4 to learn how to enter the presence of God and for the manifestation of the spirit to happen. We had just been practicing enjoying Jesus, worshipping and adoring Him. I then saw as one person next to me was kneeling and lifting their hands, a circle of energy appeared in front of them. A big circle filled with pulsating bluish, white light. It was radiant liquid energy. Eric Gilmour said, 'This is what happens when you lift your hands, a portal forms in front of you.' Then he walked over to this lady who reminded me of Mother Teresa in her humble nature. But she didn't look like her. She remained completely still for some time and she began to manifest a very large spirit bird. Eric Gilmour was very fascinated and said, 'Now when you wait on God and you are still, this is what happens, but it takes years of practice.' No one else was able to do it, only this one lady. I knew she was either some kind of nun or she was just incredibly pure. As in she had not been married and was completely given over to the Kingdom. She had greyish, white dreadlocks, long, thick and neat down to the back of her legs. When the spirit bird began to form, she was just standing still 'waiting on God'. The bird was flying and twirling around in front of her. It was much bigger than she was, and it was filled with much more liquid energy than the previous circle/portal. It was absolutely beautiful, and everyone was stunned. The lady seemed to disappear, and her spirit stepped backwards out of her body and flew upwards into the flow of the liquid energy bird and became one. She was clearly enjoying it. Then she stepped back into her body with all the liquid energy flowing into her. She walked to the rest of the crowd by the other people, full of excitement and exclaimed, 'This is definitely Kingdom!'.

I'll end the dream there, even though there was a bit more, since it was more personal pertaining to my calling. So, this 2nd dream shows us what actually happens when we lift our hands, and when we wait on the Lord. How beautiful is it to know that our spirit and the Holy Spirit join to become one and the life force of Holy Spirit flows into us having twirled and whirled in a dance with Him in the spirit. And what's even more beautiful is that this is all just the starting point!

Activation

See what other prophetic revelation you receive from God as you re-read through the dream. The more I read through my dreams the more revelation I get. Make sure to always write your dreams down and re-visit them from time to time so that the Lord can expound on them.

Don't rely on music. Learn to worship without it. It must come from your heart and not merely because you are following along with songs. If you feel like listening to worship music, there is no harm though, in using different soaking tracks to discover for yourself how your prophetic flow reacts while in stillness before God. Do you get more visions, or check-out into the spirit faster? Or do you simply feel the peace of God with some music tracks. Practice setting the Lord before you by imagining being with Him and be in adoration of Him as you drift into bliss with Him. But never let music be the foundation. Your foundation is Jesus alone, music is just a tool to worship and engage God by

TRUTH and SPIRIT, use your own words from your heart, not only the lyrics of the songs!

Try getting up at 3am to pray, note how big of a difference it is and you will learn to fall in love with it.

Prayer

Father help me to learn to wait upon you with diligence and patience. May I learn to pray the way that Jesus prayed, in spirit and in truth. Give me abundance of grace to stop all striving and simply rest in your embrace as I enter into divine unity with you. I humbly ask to increase your presence over my life and prayer life. Meet with me in the secret place as I seek after you, for I believe that I will find you as I seek you with all my heart. Come to me, send your saints and angels to teach me. I invite the hosts of Heaven into my life. Thank You for the ability to have this relationship with You Jesus, Amen!

11

Conclusion

In this book I have given insights into the life of a prophet and the means in which people may develop their prophetic abilities through intimacy with our loving Heavenly Father. No person has come to the fullness of their gifting or will in this lifetime, if you did you would only be able to gain just enough to be like Enoch and transcend space and time to walk in the Heavenly Realms with God. Our goal should never be to do that, but instead it should be to come into a transfigured state as Jesus did. If we fully understand who and what we are we will walk in the glorified (resurrected body) of Jesus because we were justified and raised up as one with Christ.

The prophetic is a process, there is no condemnation if you get it wrong and are humble about it, but for those that are falsely prophetic for the sake of fame or being noticed already have their reward.

I pray that you grow in love and relationship with God so that you will be able to hear the heart of God for all people. May your spiritual eyes and ears be opened, and may you have a discerning heart to judge unto life and not death.

God is a loving Father so don't be afraid of making mistakes along the way, it is important to make mistakes so that we can develop humility in the process.

Use the tools of a prophet to stir up the prophetic gifts within you and be diligent in applying the blood of Christ over the gateways of your soul so that you may function freely. Remember who you are and the authority you carry is one with God's. God Bless!

12

Bonus Chapter: The Latter Rain Church

We will be a nameless, faceless church, all as one in unity representing the head which is Christ Jesus. We will walk in the supernatural to such an extent that miracles that we couldn't even fathom will begin happening before our eyes. We will see such new things that we could never say I knew such things or have heard of such things. Indeed it will go beyond our wildest expectations as we begin to engage new realities of the Kingdom of Heaven.

'You have heard; See all this. And will you not declare it? I have made you hear new things from this time, Even hidden things, and you did not know them. They are created now and not from the beginning; And before this day you have not heard them, Lest you should say, 'Of course I knew them.'' (Isaiah 48:6-7 NKJV)

'Do not remember the former things, Nor consider the things of old. Behold, I will do a new thing, Now it shall spring forth; Shall you not know it? I will

even make a road in the wilderness And rivers in the desert.' (Isaiah 43:18-19 NKJV)

With great periods of sufferings must come great periods of prosperity. As in the case with Joseph who stored grain for 7 years during a time of great prosperity, so we too need to pay attention to the times and seasons. Depending on when you are reading this book, you may be at the beginning of the changes, or you may be in the middle and seeing the final harvest. I assure you, that you have a part to play. Ask and the Lord will use you. Especially now since prophets have risen to the forefront and a new breed of seers have come about, which are the 'complete prophets' who walk in all functionality! Know that your part to play as a forerunner is one that must be focused on the protection of the people of God. For those that are slow to learn and are hard of heart, be patient and pray diligently that we may all come to the full knowledge of the love of the Beloved Son of God. And pray earnestly that your Christian communities, especially hidden ones may be protected and provided for by one another. With the mark of the beast coming, you will need to be able to hear the ever proceeding word of God to be able to live in the last days. New inventions from the children of God will come forth. If you as a seer, are given the opportunity to receive ideas that can help others, especially in the area of bartering, please be diligent in bringing forth those concepts. We will not be able to use money so teach it with all diligence because the hope that you have others do not have. And as ones carrying the hope of the glory of God, we must be bolder, wiser and sharper than the world.

Love with all diligence, forsaking all opinions and selfish ambition, do everything for the sake of the Kingdom of God and for God's children. If you have an abundance of anything at all, provide it for those that do not have. Especially if the Lord has given you an oversupply of anything, use it as a means of either giving freely or bartering within reasonable and loving intentions. We need to provide a means to aid those without jobs since there will be a great persecution and discrimination against Christians. There is a significant need to teach people how to run their own businesses now that we are in the information age. What will you do when all Christians can no longer work because they refuse the vaccines and mark of the beast instead of following the new world government? Education will only be given to those who have been vaccinated with microchips. Healthcare and jobs will only be given to those who have the mark or vaccinated as well. If you are too old and think you may not be around for that, consider all that I have spoken about in this book. You are called for immortality and eternal life as we profess the word of God and the faith that we hold on to. Jesus' return is imminent!

You may not agree because you have grown up with a different mindset. But I firmly believe that the best thing for us as children of God is to study the word of God as our source of education and reliance upon the Holy Spirit as our teacher from now onwards. Schools will not teach your children the truth of the word of God, especially schools depending on government finance. The agenda is to manipulate your children's thoughts to believe everything contradictory to the word of God so you must take responsibility in training your children the way that they should go by yourself and with the help of Holy Spirit. These children carrying the purity of the Kingdom combined with ideas from Heaven will transform this world and they will be able to rule and reign with Christ for the 1000 years spoken about in Revelations. That time is around the corner!

Be bold, save as many people as you can. We may get beheaded for the gospel, but if you are willing to believe it. You will be unaffected, able to enjoy the powers of the age to come and walking in all authority, power and dominion with Christ. You will have the power over death itself, and the ability to take up your own life again. That means this new transfigured state is available for us now! Press in, give yourself over to be devoted to the Lord and the works of God.

'But seek first the Kingdom of God and His righteousness, and all these things shall be added to you.' (Matthew 6:33 NKJV)

False Prophets of the End Times

In days to come it is important to recognise who are false prophets. Many will arise claiming that they are the Christ. Being one with Christ and calling yourself 'the Christ' are two different things.

'For false christs and false prophets will rise and show great signs and wonders to deceive, if possible, even the elect.' (Matthew 24:24 NKJV)

How do we discern whether a prophet is a true prophet from God or is a hypocritical play actor? Prophets will always seek to glorify God, they do not seek to glorify themselves, in fact God glorifies and justifies Himself through them! God Himself will show up with signs and wonders to back up and confirm the words that come from His prophet's mouth. Jesus says that a prophet is without honour in His own hometown (John 4:44). That means we should actually pay attention to their life and their backstory and whether it continues to hold true. As I explained earlier that a prophet will always have had to deal with rejection from the ones closest to them before being recognised by the public eye, away from whom they usually associate with.

'When He had come to His own country, He taught them in their synagogue, so that they were astonished and said, "Where did this Man get this wisdom and these mighty works? Is this not the carpenter's son? Is not His mother called Mary? And His brothers James, Joses, Simon, and Judas? And His sisters, are they not all with us? Where then did this Man get all these things?" So they were offended at Him. But Jesus said to them, "A prophet is not without honour except in his own country and in his own house." Now He did not do many mighty works there because of their unbelief.' (Matthew 13:54-58 NKJV)

Prophets will usually end up like Jonah fleeing away from their calling until they realise that they are meant to be a prophet and commit themselves to the will of God. Until then, God will rock the boat! And either you jump overboard, or you will get thrown overboard. People who have been handed everything on a silver platter without the humbling/humiliation process in their own hometown will never be able to relate to all people, wherever the Lord sends them or in whatever way the Lord requires them to be used. So, when riches, fame or respect does come because of the fire, honour can be given its rightful place and glory may be pointed towards God.

Fortunately, we can all be prophetic, but prophets are born not made. Good well-meaning people can easily be mistaken by hopeful wishing to be a prophet because they think it is something of high regard and will gain them fame or more respect. This is not the case since prophets usually never know that they are one until life changing supernatural events take place. That means you can't aim to be one, but you can grow tremendously in the prophetic and gain insight like prophets do. God has given prophets the specific instruction of carrying the testimony of our Lord Jesus Christ.

Real prophets usually wish they were not prophets and don't have a one-size-fits-all formula to hear or see what they want to receive from God and so must rely on intimacy with God to hear what He is saying in order to relay messages to others or govern their life. But at the foundation they love God, trust Him and live a life of 'Not my will be done, but yours'. So, a prophet's heart attitude would really be 'It's ok, I will suffer for the Kingdom and for the glory of God', even while their flesh may cry wishing things didn't have to go this way. Most often they wish that they could get normal jobs and live a normal life with a family like everyone else.

A false prophet will always proclaim peace when there is no peace! So you will notice that false prophets will always play with words, seeking to look smarter or better by upping one encouraging word over another to be a people pleaser, without seeking the edification of the church body to bring them up to unity as flawless manifested 'Sons of God'. Prophets will always seek to protect and love rather than simply point out flaws. Anyone can point out people's flaws, but it takes God in a man to see into the Kingdom realm and bring out the gold in another.

A simple truth is that false prophets are not in love with Jesus! You will know a prophet by his intimacy and desire for God as well as his sharp, corrective words done with the sincerest heart of love. They are always misunderstood by people, thinking they are offensive when they are calling people to a higher state. Although they can be harsh when needed to be, but only at evil! As Elijah killed the false prophets of baal and Jesus created a whip and drove out the money changers in the temple and pigs (symbolic of unclean spirits) so too will true prophets be unafraid to hold back truth in order to protect God's people. This of which is done truly to bring people into their highest calling rather than sugar-coat encouraging words without any reprimand of sin. False prophets will say 'its ok, grace will cover you' and let you keep on sinning. True prophets understand that grace is meant to empower you to stop sinning. That doesn't mean that you or they don't have the ability to sin, it means that they are continually promoting God's grace that is available to empower us to live free from sin. Prophets will seek the highest truth! That we are one with God in Christ and therefore have an attitude of 'how can we take the body of God and sin with it or even utter immoral, degrading words'. With such sharp words, they will always speak but leave room for Holy Spirit to convict a man and turn them from the error of their ways, no matter how long it may take. Love is at the forefront. Patience and due diligence are the prophet's best weapons.

In the days to come, test the prophets to see what they say is from God. The fastest way to do that is to develop your relationship with God to such an extent that you will be able to discern by the intuitiveness from the Holy Spirit rather than using natural reasoning to judge prophets. The carnal mind is always at enmity against God!

Learn To Barter

Since there will be a time that we will no longer be able to buy and sell, it is important that we learn how to barter amongst our Christian brothers and sisters. Are you able to grow different foods or vegetables? What about your talents, can you use them to help someone in return for provisions?

Consider now that we have stepped into the latter days and new inventions and technology are coming to the forefront. We need to learn to adapt and begin to create our own wealth so that we can help others fulfil their earthly assignment and bring the gospel to the nations! How could you live without money?

How can you use your prophetic giftings to be an asset to the people around you? Your unique blueprints that God has kept in store for you in Heaven is waiting for you to take full responsibility for. These are important things to consider when a new era comes in. Before the coming of our Lord Jesus Christ we will need to work while it is still day because no man can work while it is night! (John 9:4)

Learn as much as you can, as fast you can! Love, protect and warn those you are able to. Wickedness will increase in the last days, but the Lord has much in store for His children if they desire it!

OTHER BOOKS, COURSES & PROGRAMS BY KURSHIN JOSEPH

Available Resources at Heavens Digital Academy:

heavensdigitalacademy .com

>1K Accelerator Program
School of The Kingdom Leader
Kingdom Entrepreneur - The Ultimate Leader Machine
FREE: Spiritual Transformation Series

Available at Kurshin Joseph

kurshinjoseph .com

Online Business Coaching/Strategy Sessions
FREE: Prophetic Ministry Sessions
FREE: Automated Income Secrets

Media

Kingdom Discovery Channel
Heavens Entrepreneurs Podcast
YouTube - Interviews, Teachings, Prophetic Updates & More

Join Our Kingdom Family Tribe: Heavens Entrepreneurs
Regular Meetings / Networking and Kingdom Family Teaching/Prayer Sessions

About The Author
"I am His!"

E-commerce Empire Builder, Founder of Heavens Digital Academy & Heavens Entrepreneurs, Kingdom Entrepreneur, Prophetic Voice and Author of Rise of The Seer Prophets & Creator of best selling business & ministry programs, Australian entrepreneur & ministry speaker Kurshin Joseph is on a mission to raise Kingdom Leaders and call the sons of God into their prophetic calling by equipping them to expand the Kingdom through their business, life and ministry in the New Day.

JOIN OUR KINGDOM FAMILY!

HEAVENS DIGITAL ACADEMY
RAISING KINGDOM LEADERS

Empowering You To Become A Kingdom Leader And Manifest Into A Mature Son of God

Learn more at **heavensdigitalacademy.com**

Watch **Becoming Godfident** to become an adamant, bold and confident son of God! *Available on the Kingdom Discovery Channel*

Watch Kingdom Entrepreneur / Supernatural Ministry Interviews, Kingdom Teachings and More on the Kingdom Discovery Channel

Do you enjoy listening to Podcasts on the go?

LISTEN TO HEAVEN'S ENTREPRENEURS ON YOUR FAVOURITE PODCAST CHANNEL FOR PROPHETIC UPDATES AND KINGDOM ENTREPRENEURSHIP TALKS AND INTERVIEWS!

Learn More At kurshinjoseph.com